# HIDDEN JOURNEY

# ANDREW HARVEY

HENRY HOLT
AND COMPANY
NEW YORK

# HIDDEN JOURNEY

A SPIRITUAL AWAKENING

Published by Henry Holt and Company, Inc.,
115 West 18th Street, New York, New York 10011.
Published in Canada by Fitzhenry & Whiteside Limited,
195 Allstate Parkway, Markham, Ontario L3R 4T8.

Library of Congress Cataloging-in-Publication Data
Harvey, Andrew.
Hidden journey : a spiritual awakening / Andrew Harvey.—
1st ed.
p.    cm.
ISBN 0-8050-1454-3 (alk. paper)
1. Harvey, Andrew.    2. Meera, Mother, 1960–
3. Spiritual life.    4. Religious biography.    I. Title.
BL73.H37A3    1991
828'.91409—dc20                                90-5157
[B]                                                    CIP

Henry Holt books are available at special discounts
for bulk purchases for sales promotions, premiums,
fund-raising, or educational use. Special editions
or book excerpts can also be created to specification.
For details contact:
Special Sales Director, Henry Holt and Company, Inc.
115 West 18th Street, New York, New York 10011

*First Edition*

BOOK DESIGN BY CLAIRE NAYLON VACCARO

Printed in the United States of America
Recognizing the importance of preserving
the written word, Henry Holt and Company, Inc.,
by policy, prints all of its first editions
on acid-free paper. ∞

1   3   5   7   9   10   8   6   4   2

FOR MOTHER MEERA

Heart, you are lost: but there's a path
From the lover to love, hidden
But visible. Worlds blaze round you.
Don't shrink; the path's hidden, but yours.

—RUMI

I approached near unto hell, even to the gates of Proserpina,
and after that I was ravished throughout all the elements, and
I returned to my proper place: about midnight I saw the sun
brightly shine.

—*The Golden Ass*, APULEIUS

# LORD
# MOTHER

# ONE

Once, my mother tells me, when I was a child of three in India I ran into her room and shouted "There's a funny lady in the garden." I stuck out my tongue, pulled my face out of shape, and stood on one leg. My mother had no idea what I was trying to tell her until she remembered: in the garden next door stood a scowling many-armed granite statue of Kali, the Divine Mother.

One of the first photographs of me is of a spindly, bony boy trying to reproduce Kali's stance in the doorway of our house in Nagpur.

In the hilly, snake-infested wilderness behind our house in Old Delhi there were hundreds of wild peacocks. If you walked there at dusk, the air would be ringing with their sudden screams and you would see them stalking and spreading their fans under almost every tree.

"She must come here often," my ayah used to say.

"Who?"

"Ma, the Goddess. She loves peacocks."

"Can we see her?"

"If you saw her, you would die."

Several times in dreams I saw two pitch-black eyes, vast as suns, staring at me as I wandered among the peacocks.

"Why are the eyes so big?" I asked my ayah.

"Because everything is in them," she said, looking down at her hands.

"Where is the Goddess?" I asked my ayah one morning. She looked startled.

"The Goddess is everywhere."

"Then why can't I see her?"

She looked out the window.

"Can I see her and not die?" I asked after a while.

"Only if you are very lucky."

"I will see her," I said loudly, "and I will live. You wait and see."

"No need to shout." She chuckled. "Ma can hear."

In India the miraculous is commonplace, so when I was told at six by my favorite aunt, B, who lived in the apartment upstairs, that a saint was going to visit her that afternoon—a woman who had died and come back to life again—I was curious, not skeptical.

I am not sure what I expected to see when I entered B's bedroom, but it was not two old women lying on the bed laughing and eating chocolates. I had imagined saints would always be in trance; I had not imagined one would sprawl on a bed, enormous in her white cotton sari, looking very much like any other worn and plump old Indian woman.

"Come onto the bed," B said, "and lie down between us."
I climbed up onto the bed gingerly.

The saint gave me a vast toothless smile and produced from the folds of her sari a chocolate, which she opened and held out to me.

"Oh," she sighed, "I am *too* fond of chocolates." She smelled of biscuits and incense and played with my ears.

"What big ears you have. This is good. The Buddha had big ears. I, too, have big ears."

She lifted a strand of dank white hair and showed me her ears. They were huge and ugly.

"Shantih knows everything there is to know," B said. "Her name means peace. She has seen God. She sees God all the time. Ma is a great saint and thousands worship her and she has done many miracles."

"Have you really done miracles?" I asked.

"They come through me like water through a pipe. But the water is not mine."

"Where does the water come from?"

She yawned slightly, pointed upward.

"Have you really died and come back to life, and did you see God?"

B laughed, got off the bed, and went into the bathroom to have a bath.

"You want to know?" Shantih asked.

"Yes," I said, feeling frightened.

She stroked my cheek dreamily with one of her fingers and said, "God is gentle, gentle as my finger."

"About seventy years ago," she went on, "I was another person, a woman, living in a North Indian village, married with several children. I got ill and died. When I died, a light came to me, and in it I saw my Lord Krishna. This is what will happen to you, too, when you die. A light will come and you will see whoever you believe in. If you believe in Krishna, you will see him; if you are a Christian, you will see Christ. From this light

Krishna spoke to me. 'You have loved me in your life,' he said, 'and I love you and will give you liberation. But you must go down to the earth and tell them what you have experienced so humans can lose their fear of death and love me more.' I did not want to come down here again; I wanted to be there with him in the Light; but gods are strong, you know, and you have to do what they tell you. So I came back."

She said all this as if she were describing the train schedule to Agra or giving shopping instructions to the ayah.

She said, "Go and close the curtains. I will show you something."

I did as I was told.

Shantih leaned over, wheezing a little, and switched on the light by the bed. The swirling red and gold dragons on the lampshade that had been dull a moment before flared into life.

She clapped her hands.

"In everything and everyone the Light is shining. It is not like this light. It is softer. It is everywhere."

"Is it in me?"

"It is in you and all around you and in everyone and around everyone and everything. Without it nothing could exist. It is God."

"Do you see this light?"

"Yes." She laughed. "I see this Light always. You, too, can see it. It is simple. God is simple; we are complicated."

She turned the lamp off. I opened the curtains, and sun flooded the room. I turned to Shantih. She was seated on the bed in meditation, immense and calm, a half-unwrapped chocolate on her lap.

ॐ An old Indian poet once said to me, "India is mad with all the madness of reality. Splendor and terror, violence and mystery coexist here—two faces of one eternal Kali."

To have had an Indian childhood is to have been initiated very young into horror as well as miracle. I had only to look out of the car window to see the fingerless lepers in the streets, the poor huddled under patchwork blankets in midwinter, the old women hardly able to walk dragging pails of water or working on building sites in blinding sun. My grandmother's shaved and colonnaded garden was full of snakes that the snake man caught and threw, hissing, into a gunnysack; a Russell's viper I saw one morning glittering at the bottom of the garden well killed two cows and a child. One night when my parents had gone to a party I lay in their bed and listened to a howling that sounded like the misery of all India rising to the night sky. Next morning I saw a thin, brown rabid dog being strapped to the back of a bicycle, its mouth a mop of blood and foam. Its terrible face appeared in my dreams for years.

Most of my childhood was lived in a house on Alipur Road in Old Delhi. The Turkish and Moghul tombs nearby and the abandoned British residences even then starting to crumble taught me that history was a game decay always won. My first paintings were of tombs and my first poems drenched with the easy pathos of vanished grandeur. When I first visited London at seven, I saw in my mind's eye cows grazing around Nelson's column as they graze around the Kutb Minar. My ayah used to sing an old Hindi song: "All things pass away except God/ O my God show me your face before I die."

ॐ When I was five years old, I escaped one afternoon from my parent's house while everyone was asleep and went for a walk by the river Jamuna.

Under a tree, seated on a filthy dark blue cloth, I saw a yogi. He was emaciated, with long knotted gray hair, and naked except for a loincloth. He waved to me to come and sit next to him with such a beautiful wild smile that I lost all fear.

There were two objects on the cloth by him—a tiny statue of a woman with several arms, and something wrapped in a red rag that looked like a small loaf. He pointed to the statue and said, "Ma. This Ma."

Then he pointed to his forehead. "In here, Ma. In here, God." He pointed to his body: "Body is house. House of Ma. Ma is head of house. Ma is big chief of house." He started to rock forward and backward with his eyes closed murmuring something. Then he picked up some of the white sand of the Jamuna riverbank.

"This sand, Ma. This river, Ma. This light, this foot, everything, Ma. Understand? Everything same, same. One thing. One thing," he kept repeating. "All Ma. Dog Ma, plant Ma."

He leaned forward and touched my nose. "You, too, Ma."

Then he reached out for the object wrapped in the red cloth by his side. He unwrapped it slowly. It was an old skull.

He took my right hand in his and rubbed it gently on top of the skull.

"No afraid," he said softly. "Death also Ma. Life death same thing. You me same thing. Only one thing. Only Ma."

ॐ "India is mad with all the madness of reality," the old poet said. The snake man laughs as he swirls the bag of writhing killers around his head; the maharani sighs and adjusts her pearls as she passes the starving child; the twilight sun streaks the feathers of the murdered peacocks in the back of the Jeep full of tobacco smoke. An awareness of violent contradiction and paradox entered my imagination early and pervaded it. Western rationalizations or secular dreams of progress, however much I tried to share them, were always foreign to me, as were all versions of the Divine that left out terror and destruction. My inner reality was of the skinned panther on my father's veranda, and the mango lying on a silver plate near it, the lapis lazuli lozenges glittering in the doorways of Moghul ruins and the beggars coughing under them, the deer's body I found once in a garden in the Nilgiri hills lying eviscerated, swarming with ants, under a light-riddled display of jacaranda.

When I was six years old, I went on a holiday with my grandmother to the sea, to Mangalore in the south. I remember a golden beach, curving in the sun, and an island about a hundred yards from shore, deserted and paradisal, dense with palms.

I was lying on a towel half-asleep when my grandmother staggered screaming out of the sea and fell on the beach. My uncle ran to her, knelt down, and starting sucking at her left ankle, sucking and spitting out blood onto the sand. She had been lashed by a stingray.

All at once there was no safety anywhere.

My grandmother lay under a mosquito net for three days. I sat by her watching the sweat pouring down her face, talking to her when she was lucid enough to speak.

"Why did Jesus let you get hurt?"

"To test me. To see if I believed even when bad things happened."

Shantih had told me that God was as gentle as her finger; but God also let the stingray almost kill my grandmother.

"Why is there pain?"

"Pain teaches you not to trust the body or the world."

"What do you trust, then?"

"The spirit. God." She clutched her side and could not speak.

"One day," she moaned to herself, "all this will be over."

Not long after, my mother left me at boarding school a thousand miles away from where we lived.

I hardly remember my father in my childhood; my reality was my mother. I loved her with a devotion that was inseparable from my love of India, from the asphalt-and-jasmine smell of the night when she left for a party, from the fragrance of the roses open by her bed when I crawled into it in the mornings. My head rang with the legends of old India, of saints who had given up everything to wander the hot plains singing God's name, of princes who had died for the love of princesses, of Shāh Jāhan, who had built the Taj Mahal and studded it with the rubies and emeralds of an empire for the love of his wife; I wanted to enact for my mother this prodigal and gorgeous adoration. She and India were my two enchantments and she, in her dark beauty and sense of passion, seemed to me a figure from an ancient world, a queen of Golconda or Maabar, out of place in a life of mah-jongg and lazy afternoon trips to the bazaar.

Her abandonment of me at six-and-a-half ended this fantasy forever and opened a wound that no other love, until the love this book describes, and no success or worldly happiness, could heal.

This abandonment was, I see now, a blessing. It baptized me in despair; those so baptized have no choice but to look for a final truth and its final healing, or die of inner famine.

India gave me a mother, then took her away. Years later, I found in India another Mother in another dimension, and the love I had believed lost returned. Without that first wound I would not have needed love so much or been prepared to risk everything in its search. Without the memory of a human tenderness I might never have accepted the passion that awoke in my being when I met the woman who has transformed me. From the deepest wound of my life grew its miraculous possibility.

mato sauce from a plate, listening to the cook singing in his hoarse, drink-scarred voice and beating his tabla. Each memory seemed a talisman of another reality, the proof that a dimension of freedom existed. I longed, with a physical ache, to sit with a window open to the smells and sounds of the Indian night; to feel enclosed, invaded, and possessed again by all the reality of India. Terror stalked this longing; night after night I would dream of playing cards with my mother and then going out into a night garden to be bitten by a cobra; of embracing the dalmatian I had owned as a child only to have it turn rabid. I realized that what awaited me would be as much a death as a rebirth, but over the month of waiting to leave I consented to that death. The friend who drove me to the airport tells me I said: "India is my mad mother, and I am returning to her to be made sane. I have no idea what will happen. All I know is there is nowhere and nothing else I can turn to."

I arrived in India in November 1977 and stayed in B's house in Delhi, where I had first met Shantih. For ten days I was so overwhelmed, I was unable to leave B's balcony. We sat together and watched India walk by in the streets below.

One afternoon after a large group of half-naked, ash-coated yogis had passed by, singing and dancing and stopping the traffic for miles, B said quietly: "Do you know what this country does to you? It makes you believe against your will that at any moment the curtain of what you have called reality can part and reveal something amazing, fabulous. The revelation has not come. But I am patient."

The wild, plangent singing of the yogis drifted back to us through the dusk. B turned to me. "Revelation will come to you. I have always known that. Ever since you were a child. Once I asked you what you wanted to be. Do you remember what you said?"

I shook my head.

B laughed. "You said you wanted to be a singer or a saint. I knew then the world would not be enough for you. This country had bitten you too deep."

"But I am not looking for a revelation," I said.

"You don't look for *it*. It finds *you*."

Three months later I found myself in the south of India, in Pondicherry, a former French colonial town on the sea, visiting the ashram of Aurobindo. I had not heard of Aurobindo or Pondicherry before I came back to India; I had no intentions of visiting any ashrams (four years' experience at an Oxford college had cured me of any fascination with "monasticism"). I went there on a whim, on a chance remark from a fellow traveler who had found me thin and depressed in a fleapit in Tanjore and said, "Go to Pondy and get yourself a supply of good English beer, French bread, and a clean room."

My first days in Pondicherry—despite the English beer, French bread, and clean room—were disgruntled. The city itself unnerved me with its long, straight, empty avenues baking in unwaveringly harsh sun. I disliked the ashram with its pompous colonial buildings and air of goody-goody white-washed piety. What little I gleaned of Aurobindo's philosophy of evolution struck me as ridiculous. I wrote to a friend in England who had been afraid I would "get religion" in India that Aurobindo was obviously an escapee from reality, a fantasist of the most grandiose proportions. How could anyone but a fantasist believe at this moment that humankind had any hope of saving itself, let alone "leaping into Divine Being," or some such rubbish, after the Gulags, the First and Second World Wars? After Hiroshima and Auschwitz, Kampuchea and Vietnam? As for sweet Mother, his Shakti, the half-French half-Turkish sibyl who had accompanied him on his "adventure," I wrote: "I see nothing in the so-called Mother of the Universe and Cocreator of the coming transformation of human beings into divine infants but an ancient Jewess with an appalling taste in clothes." I ended the letter: "I am leaving this incense-scented morgue tomorrow for the beach (*any* beach *anywhere*) and a little sensual sanity. I'd rather die drunk in a Calcutta ditch than spend another day here."

In fact, I went on to spend four more months.

That evening I met Jean-Marc Frechette and began a friendship that would change my life.

🕉 He was standing in front of me in the ashram food queue, frail, stooped, with balding light chestnut hair and large, slightly protruding eyes, reading Jaccottet's translations of Hopkins. I was so relieved to see someone reading and not wandering in the usual ashram daze that I moved close to him and craned over his shoulder. We started talking and continued most of the night. He was from Montreal and lived in a guest house near the ashram. He loved Rilke, Piero della Francesca, and Callas, as I did; we had a whole culture in common, and that bound us immediately. But he had made a transition into the Eastern world that I had not managed.

"Why are you here?" I asked him.

"To change my life."

"You believe in Aurobindo's philosophy?"

"Belief is not so important. What is important is experience. I experience his philosophy."

That made me furious. As we walked by the sea I launched into a denunciation of the escapism of ashrams in general and the uselessness of Eastern wisdom in the face of the problems of the world.

"The world is in its last nightmare, and sweet old clichés like 'peace of mind' and 'the power of meditation' and 'evolution into divine being' aren't going to wake it up. So-called Eastern wisdom is as bankrupt and helpless as that of the West—more so, in fact, because its claims are so much more grandiloquent."

Jean-Marc heard me out with barely suppressed amusement.

"Why don't you just let go of it?" he said.

"Let go of what?"

"The toy you are holding."

"Don't be cryptic."

"You are holding on to horror and tragedy like a child on to its last toy. It is all you have left, the last rags of a costume you do not want to give up."

His certainty exploded me into another tirade. "I'd rather die than be calm. I'd rather die of the horror I see everywhere than hide from it in some smug yogic catatonia."

Jean-Marc dropped to the sand laughing.

"Oh, my god," he said, wiping his eyes. "No wonder you like Callas so much."

He imitated my indignant face and flailing arms.

"You see the world as one long grim nineteenth-century opera with nothing in it but pain and loss. You refuse to imagine anything but catastrophe."

He started laughing again. "How conventional."

"Stop laughing, damn you!"

"I don't have to stop laughing. *You* have to start. Don't you see how absurd you are being? Look around you. Feel this night, its sweetness, the softness of the sand where we are walking. You've been running from your spirit for years. You must stop. You must sit down, shut up, open, listen, and wait. Give your soul a chance to breathe. Never in my life have I seen a performance such as the one you have just given. The only thing you *didn't* do is cut open a vein."

He stood up and put his arm around me. "The room next

to mine in the guest house is vacant tomorrow. Why don't you take it? We could go on talking and walking by the sea. I could introduce you to my poetic genius, and we could drink tea in the garden in the afternoon like old British colonels."

Undoing a year's careful planning, I accepted.


🕉 Jean-Marc's gift to me—for which I will always be grateful—was to live the spiritual life before my eyes with such a happy simplicity I could not deny its truth. Jean-Marc had given up all "normal" life for a small room with a badly working fan by the sea in South India. He had almost no money, no job to go to, no ring of friends to sustain his choice—nothing, in fact, but his faith, his few books of Claudel, Rene Char, and Aurobindo, and the sound of the sea. Yet he was the clearest man I had ever known, spare, joyful, delightfully eccentric, like his room with its narrow, lopsided wooden bed, its desk with one leg propped up by an old copy of the Upanishads, its cracked blue china bowl kept always full of flowers. Nothing interested him less than preaching his mystic insights; he lived them, writing them down in huge swirling letters in the garden swept by sea wind, reading Meister Eckhart and John of the Cross, swigging tea from a flask, walking up and down the beach in his loping zigzag gait, his eyes brilliant with mischief and hilarity. Jean-Marc never talked about renunciation or expiation; although he had been brought up a Quebecois Catholic in a country village, he detested all notions of guilt and original sin—"how vulgar to imagine that God cannot forgive anything"; "this world is divine," he would repeat again and again, leaning down to stroke the beach like an old dog or ruffling the long grass with closed eyes. "Hopkins was right: 'There lives the dearest freshness deep down things.' You just have to go deep enough to find it and to stay with it."

"Your problem," he would say, lowering his voice conspiratorially, "is that, like so many postromantics, you find suffering glorious. Pain has become your substitute for religion. But pain is not glorious; it is boring. Joy is glorious. Praise is glorious. Because they are hard. You have to work at them with your whole being. Your other problem is that you want— like almost every other intellectual Westerner I have ever met—to do everything yourself. You think there is something 'unmanly' in asking anyone else for help, let alone looking for a Master who could guide you. Meister Eckhart said: 'A fly in God is greater than an angel in himself.' You are a vain angel."

Slowly Jean-Marc persuaded me to go with him to the ashram, to visit Aurobindo's tomb, to examine my earlier dismissal of meditation. One day he said, "Why don't you just sit by Aurobindo's tomb and see what happens?" I sat day after day with the other silent meditators by the white slab heaped with lotuses and jasmine. Nothing happened; I just felt hot, sad, and angry at the confusion in my mind.

Then, one afternoon, just as I had decided to leave and get some tea, the thoughts that had been racing through my brain were suddenly silenced. I felt my entire being gasp for joy, a kind of joy I had never before experienced. I did not tell Jean-Marc for fear that if I talked about the experience it would vanish—but it repeated with more or less the same intensity for days afterward.

At last I told him.

"Well . . . " Jean-Marc smiled. "Now you know that the power of meditation is not a 'sweet old cliché.' Your new life is starting."

We went to the Hôtel de Ville on the seafront and celebrated with one tepid bottle of beer each. Later, as we sat on the beach under a nearly full moon, he wrote out one of his poems for me in the sand:

O moon
Mingle our quiet tears
With the tail of comets . . .
For so the soul begins.

Now Jean-Marc began to lay before me the visionary treasures of his inner life. I listened astonished as he told me of a vision he had had in Duino Castle when Aurobindo had appeared to him in the middle of a lotus of fire; a week before I would have been tempted to dismiss this as fantasy, but now each detail seemed essential, a key to a new possibility.

"Mystics are not special human beings," Jean-Marc said. "Each human being is a special kind of mystic. Not everyone, however, wants to know this or to find out what it means. Those who do, and who become conscious of their inner power, see and know as clearly as you and I see this rose or the sea outside the window."

I still had no real idea what he was talking about. Experiences of the next few weeks would sweep that ignorance away.

Every day I meditated before sleep and soon began to hear a low hum coming from all around me, the walls, the flowers, the sound of the sea itself. If I tried too hard to concentrate on it, it would go away. When I let my mind rest, it would surround me. I told Jean-Marc.

"Good," he said. "So that is beginning."

I pressed him.

"Creation has a sound. You are hearing it, or part of it."

One night, about a week after I had been hearing the sound, I had the first vision of my life, which overturned everything I had known up until then.

I fell asleep but I did not feel it like sleep at all. I was simply at peace, detached from my body, which I could see lying beneath me. Rapidly, as if in a great wind, I found myself taken to a white room, open to sounds of the afternoon, in which Aurobindo himself was sitting, white-haired, calm, surrounded by a group of silent disciples. The room was not his room in Pondicherry, which I had seen, but one more ancient. I felt as if I were in ancient India. Nothing was said; I moved toward Aurobindo naturally, as if to a long-lost father. I put my head in his lap, and he rested one hand on it.

Then I entered a cloud of swirling light. The Light was filled with thousands and thousands of voices, all singing in rapture. Some of the words I could make out, some were in languages I knew, some in languages I had never heard before. I heard my own voice singing with them, mingling with theirs, singing the words "I hate to leave you, but it is your will and I must go down." I did not know what the words meant, but my heart was filled with an immense love for the Light I was mingled with. Having to leave it filled me with grief; my voice burned and rose and fell with the others.

The music stopped. I found myself bound, almost choking, in a dark chute hurtling down what seemed like a long slide. Then, with a bump, I hit ground and woke up.

I heard the words distinctly, spoken in a calm male voice: "Remember who you are. Remember where you come from."

My body was flooded with waves of blissful energy that swept up and down into the pulse and rhythm of the music I had heard.

As soon as I could collect myself, I went out into the

morning, lay in the long grass of the garden, and wept with gratitude.

Then fear began. Was I going mad? What would I *do* with this new, overwhelming knowledge? How would I always remember who I am and where I came from? I knew I had been graced with a great insight, but what would I *do* with it?

"What do you *do*?" Jean-Marc laughed. "You get down on your knees and say a hundred thousand thank-yous for a start. Then you wait."

*"Wait?"* I exploded.

Jean-Marc broke into wild laughter. "Two weeks ago you denied enlightenment existed. Now you want to be enlightened instantly. Some people work and wait years for what you have just been given, and here you are already demanding everything. Go on meditating; be calm. And, for God's sake, enjoy yourself."

Even after my vision I avoided reading Aurobindo seriously. I had an intuition that I would have to be taught inwardly how to read him, that if I read him too soon and with an unripe, defensive, or merely curious mind, I would miss the immediacy of his vision. All my life I had thought myself intelligent enough to understand anything: now I realized how limited my understanding of intelligence had been. Nothing in my Western training could help me explore what I had begun to see; now I knew only enough to know I would have to trust and be led forward by whatever Power was educating me.

In the following weeks of quiet talks with Jean-Marc and meditation by Aurobindo's tomb, I began to see how much of my inner life my mind had been repressing or denying. A thousand memories of my Indian childhood returned in their old wide happiness: I began to connect the joys I had known in music and friendship and in a few moments of lovemaking with the greater joy that was dawning in my spirit. I began to see how my fascination with the drama of my emotional life and my too-great faith in the powers of my intellect had withered my spirit. Jean-Marc had a dream of me in black, sitting at the end of a long, dark corridor, surrounded by books. "You have become imprisoned in the knowledge you acquired in order to 'become' yourself," he said to me. "Now you must let it go so another knowledge can arrive."

About a week after the first vision I was given another one in sleep, although it was more vivid than any dream.

I was sitting on one of the beaches of my childhood, the beach at Cannanore, where I had often gone in the summer holidays with my mother. In the distance I could see fishermen on their primitive boats, and the sight of their lean, tough bodies in the sun comforted me.

Something told me to look to my right. Far down the beach a figure in white was walking in my direction. As it came closer I saw the figure had a face of blinding beauty—oval, golden, with large, tender eyes. I had no idea whether the figure was male or female or both, but a love for it and a kind of high, refined desire began in me. With a shock I realized the figure was coming toward me, had, in fact, walked the length of the beach to come to me. The figure approached, sat down so close by me in the sand that I could smell its sandalwood fragrance.

I had no idea what to do. I sat with my head turned away from the figure. It said, in a soft voice, "Look at me." I turned and saw its face irradiated by a golden light that was not the light of the afternoon dancing around us on the sand but a light emanating from its eyes and skin. It put out a hand and touched my face and then cradled it.

Leaning against its breast, I experienced the most complete love for any other being I had ever felt, a love in which there was desire, but a desire so fiery and clear it filled my whole self and was focused nowhere.

Still embraced, I asked the figure, "Who are you?"

The voice came back, amused and gentle: "Who am I? Who do you think I am? I am *you*."

I fainted, and awoke.

I ran into Jean-Marc's room, although it was early, and told him.

"The Being you met is your real self," he said, "the Self liberated from all ego and irradiated by Light that you, and all of us, really are." He smiled. "Now go and pray and let me sleep."

I cycled to the ashram and leaned my forehead on the cool white stone of Aurobindo's tomb. "Lord," I found myself saying, "if it is You who are teaching me, go on. Break down all my stupidities."

It was a wonderful fresh morning, and in the great tree above the tomb the birds were singing.

"My god," I started to laugh inwardly. "If my Oxford colleagues could see me now talking out loud to a dead man, all their worst fears would be confirmed."

The thought of confirming their fears made me want to dance around the tomb.

One week later I went to Mahabalipuram, the beautiful small temple town sacred to Shiva on the west coast. I stayed alone in a small shabby room by the beach, reading the Upanishads for the first time.

I have only the most dazzled recollection of the week I spent there. The long beach, almost deserted, curved like a scimitar, and had the same smooth golden sand, the same small crabs scuttling in the warm waves, the same vast reverberation of wind and pounding sea of the beaches of my childhood. I felt restored to a world I thought lost, freed to wander again in its choiceless joy, to live in white time, where neither past nor future existed.

Two nights before I left Mahabalipuram I was strolling at midnight along the moonlit curve of beach to the hotel, when all at once my mind split apart, like a coconut thrown against a wall, and everything, instead of being deliciously and warmly outside, was now inside. The wind was inside me and the sea pounding and the sand under my feet, and the whole wild softly pulsing creation was singing with one voice OM distinctly and unmistakably, a resounding horizon-to-horizon curling, vibrant, rich OM that was sounding within me. It took whatever scrap of mind I had left to remain standing, to stagger on. There was a complete separation between whatever consciousness I was now in, seeing and reveling in this vastness, and my body tottering on the sands, barely able to hold what it had been given. I had flowered far above and around and beyond my body and was connected to it by only the most fragile of threads, only just strong enough to drag it forward, like a piece of driftwood. I had enough mind left to gaze at the hulls of the boats around me, at the nets lying on the sands, at the sands themselves, at my feet; everything was still in its old shape, but shimmering with a soft milky light. I remember, absurdly, blinking again and again to see if the vision would go away, but the roaring OM went on, and the light kept breaking from my feet and the sands around them.

Somehow I managed to get back to my hotel room.

The Upanishads were on my bedside table. I picked up the book and it fell open to the last verse of the Mandukya Upanishad: "The word *OM* as one sound is the fourth state of supreme consciousness. It is beyond the senses and is the end of evolution. It is nonduality and love. He goes with his self to the Supreme Self who knows this, who knows this."

"In Mahabalipuram you got a foretaste of bliss," Jean-Marc said, "a bite at the cake of divine knowledge. That taste of light will always be on your tongue."

"I'm scared," I said.

"Everyone is, at the beginning, and for a long time afterward." He went to the window and opened it to the warm wind from the sea. "What happened to you in Mahabalipuram is what happened to me in Duino. The first stone was broken through in the wall of the concentration camp of reason. Through the opening you can see something of the new country, the country of freedom. One day, because one stone has been taken away, another will start to crumble, then another. And then—in twenty, thirty, forty years—the whole wall will fall down and there will be no wall anymore, only that sound and that Light."

The openings I had been given and my baffled, nervous faith in them made it possible for me at last to begin to read Aurobindo with some insight. The next weeks passed in a long meditation on him. I read his major works of metaphysics, *The Divine Life*, *The Synthesis of Yoga*, *Essays on the Gita*, where he elaborates his vision of human evolution, but the book of his that most shook me was his shortest—*The Mother*.

Nothing in any of my reading or inner experience prepared me for what I found there—a vision of the Divine Mother, of God as the Mother, so radical, so potent, so all-embracing that it overturned and transformed completely everything I had hitherto understood of God. I at last found a vision of the Divine that satisfied my heart and mind and answered my profound needs—for a belief in a dynamic Feminine Power that could reshape a world I experienced as deformed by patriarchal rationalism and greed; for a relationship with the Divine that would be fearless, unpuritanical, and completely intimate, as the ideal relationship between mother and child.

"There are three ways of being of the Divine Mother of which you can become aware," Aurobindo wrote in words I memorized and repeated often. "TRANSCENDENT, the original supreme Shakti, she stands above the worlds and links the creation to the ever unmanifest mystery of the Supreme; UNIVERSAL, . . . she creates all those beings and contains and enters, supports and conducts all these million processes and forces. INDIVIDUAL, she embodies the power of these two vaster ways of her existence, makes them living and near to us and mediates between the human personality and the Divine Nature."

"But how will I really understand what Aurobindo is saying?" I asked Jean-Marc one night on the beach.

He turned to me, almost angry.

"Ask Aurobindo. Beg him for a *vision*. Don't you know yet how much he is prepared to give you?"

Then he said quietly, looking out to sea, in words that have remained with me: "This is the time of the return of the Mother. Goethe foresaw it at the end of *Faust* when Faust was redeemed by the Mothers. Ramakrishna knew it. Even the Catholics seem to know it in the increasing sacred importance they are giving to Mary. She is returning to save a tormented creation."

He paused and gazed at me. "You know something? I think she is alive."

"Who?"

"The Mother. I think she is alive."

"But Sweet Mother died in 1974."

"Another Mother," Jean-Marc said. "The Mother of the next stage of evolution. I don't know why I am saying this but lately—how amazing it would be if she *were* here somewhere and we found her and served her."

I shivered.

"Amazing—and very frightening."

Jean-Marc laughed softly.

"Bliss would conquer fear," he said.

"I don't really believe in incarnations," I said.

"Five weeks ago, *mon ami*, you didn't believe in God at all."

The day before I left to return to England I went to Aurobindo's tomb and prayed to him all day to help me understand the Mother, to give me an experience of her being.

Just as I was about to leave, sitting by his tomb in the late light, the OM sound returned and I heard: *This is the Mother's sound.*

Then immediately I saw a horizon lit up by lightnings, thousands of them, tangling and untangling like snakes. *This is the Mother's power.*

I was shocked, astounded. I walked away from the tomb to where books and photographs are sold. There was one of Sweet Mother, Aurobindo's companion, I had never seen before. She is about ninety, standing on a balcony, gazing down with ravaged compassion. My hostility to her melted. *This is the Mother's love.*

I returned, shaking, to Aurobindo's tomb.

In the air before me, as I knelt, I saw the Andromeda Nebula, blazing and turning at great speed. It took all my power of control not to leave my body.

The words came:

*I am the creation from the beginning. Everything in the creation is me. All creation is growing toward me.*

*It is begun in ecstasy.*

*It is continued in ecstasy.*

*It is sustained in ecstasy.*

*It will end in ecstasy.*

I wanted to pray to the Mother but couldn't think of any prayers to Her, except the *Ave Maria* in Latin, which I recited. Then the words began, without my willing them: "Our Mother, which art in heaven, hallowed be thy name." An extraordinary peace filled me. "Our MOTHER, which art in heaven"—just that simple change of word renewed the prayer for me, made it infinitely more tender.

I looked around at the people praying, the trees around the tomb, the incense stick, the flowers.

*All this is the Mother, and you are always in the body of the Mother.* For a second or two I felt it—that I and the marble and the flowers and the darkening tree were different softly pulsing waves of the same energy, of that, of Her.

*No separation, now or ever.*

*This is the knowledge of the Mother.*

Returning to my room, I opened Isherwood's book on Ramakrishna at these words:

> My Mother is both within and without this
> phenomenal world. . . . Giving birth to the
> world, she lives within it. She is the Spider
> and the world is the spider's web she has
> woven. . . . The spider brings the web out of
> herself and then lives in it.

 I found Jean-Marc sitting on the wall around the hotel overlooking the sea.

I told him what had happened.

"What you have experienced," he said, "is the culmination of everything you have been given in Pondicherry, the culmination and the clue."

"The clue to what?"

"We will find out."

He went on gazing calmly at the sea.

"Do you have any idea how blessed you have been? Aurobindo has taken you into the knowledge of the Mother and started to show you Her Glory. Only She knows what will happen now."

I returned to England, after seven months away, amazed and disoriented. I could tell no one what had happened without sounding ridiculous. The atmosphere of Oxford does not foster the sharing of mystical discoveries. I grew afraid both of losing what Pondicherry and Mahabalipuram had opened to me and of retaining it. What would happen if I did accept what I had seen? Where would I go? What would I do? What companions in my sophisticated and rationalist world would I find?

My fear of isolation made me realize how far I would have to explore the visions in order for them to become unshakable; made me realize, too, how great is the distance between hunger for truth and the calm of faith. In those first months of return I was compelled to face what everyone must after real visionary experience—how split I still was, how immensely split between the self that wanted worldly affirmation, sex, success, and the Self that lives in a joy beyond desire. I was ignorant of what to do now, of how to proceed in obliterating the distance between these two selves. My meditations outside India were listless. The visions of Pondicherry and Mahabalipuram remained in all their old intensity but seemed to have happened to someone else, someone who had lived for a brief rich space and then died.

This solitude grew darker in America, where I went for the first time that September of 1978, to take up a year's fellowship at Cornell. The academic game bored me; talk about

Derrida and Delleuze seemed empty after what I had begun to learn in India; the contrast between the bloodless, sardonic world of an Ivy League university and the rapture of Pondicherry grew hallucinatory. After India, America seemed a wasteland animated only by joggers and structuralists, where any talk of the spirit rang not merely absurd but comic, like expounding upon the genius of the wheel in a world of user-friendly home computers. My reaction was neurotic, but I could do nothing about it; I loathed my work, my environment, myself, even the smell of the chlorine in the university swimming pool.

Then, in the middle of November, a letter arrived from Jean-Marc that I did not open for days, out of guilt. I had not written to him for months and felt unworthy of all the time he had devoted to me, to my so-called awakening. After a particularly grim class on *Macbeth* I finally read it. It was loving and unrecriminatory. It ended with this paragraph:

> I want you to read this very carefully, to re-
> member all that happened to you in India. I
> have met someone in Pondicherry, whom I am
> certain is a Master (at the very least). A
> woman, a very young woman. I cannot say any
> more here for reasons you will understand
> when you come. You *must* come and come as
> soon as you can.

I put the letter down on the table in front of me. I picked up the phone to find out how much money I had in the bank, then went downtown and spent it all on a ticket for India, to leave on the first day of the winter break.

# TWO

"Everything in your life will change in the next month," an old astrologer I consulted in Benares said to me. He pointed to a spider's web in the corner of his shop, lit up by the sun: "You are in the web of God—you cannot get out now."

"What will change?" I pressed him.

He laughed and pointed to my dirty feet sticking out of old sandals. "Even the dust on your feet will seem different."

Jean-Marc sat swinging his legs off the end of my bed in Pondicherry. It was late Christmas Eve 1978.

"Clear your mind of everything you think you know. *Everything*. Just clear it." He made a dramatic sweeping gesture in the air. "Come to her as empty as you can, as free from every preconception."

"But who is she?"

In his excitement he had forgotten to give me any facts.

"She is seventeen years old. On the twenty-sixth of this month she will be eighteen. She lives with another Indian woman, Adilakshmi, who is in her early thirties, and a much elder man, Mr. Reddy, who is her guardian. Every day at five she gives what is called *darshan*, where you go and sit with her in silence and let her put her hands on your head and look into your eyes. She lives in a small house about a mile from here. Her name is Meera."

At the first mention of her name I started. "Meera," I said, "like *mira*—wonder, like mirror . . ."

"Meera also means miracle," Jean-Marc said, "and it is one of the holy names of the Divine Mother."

"What is she?"

Jean-Marc smiled. "You must make up your mind for yourself."

"Have you made up yours?" My voice sounded unnaturally high. Jean-Marc fell silent.


Next afternoon, Christmas Day 1978, Jean-Marc and I walked to the inconspicuous ocher-colored house near the center of Pondicherry where Meera was living. It was a brilliant day, and although I felt nervous, I was outwardly calm. We went up a narrow staircase, were ushered into the house by a plump man in a spotless white dhoti who introduced himself as Mr. Reddy and seated us with eight or nine others, mostly Indians, in a bare white room, fragrant with incense and smells of cooking. Noises of children laughing, of a Tamil radio talk show drifted up from the courtyard below through open windows. On the wall above a slightly raised, simple wooden chair with a cushion beneath it were photographs of Aurobindo and Sweet Mother. By the chair stood vases of red and purple flowers. The white cotton curtains swayed in the lazy afternoon wind, reminding me of my grandmother's house in Coimbatore.

I looked at my watch. It was two minutes to five. The silence in the room had grown charged. At five, exactly, Meera came in. I shall never forget that first sight of her. Her beauty, as she moved in a white sari through the small bead curtains, was almost disturbingly striking. Why had Jean-Marc not told me how beautiful she was? Her face and small, strong body were those of one of the goddesses in the temple sculpture of Mahabalipuram—perfectly featured, full-hipped and full-breasted, supple and subtle in every movement, every gesture. Her wrists and fingers were aristocratically thin and elegant. Her brown, deep eyes were the most startling I had ever seen— huge, molten, somehow not human, staring with calm, unblinking power through everything.

Meera sat quietly in the chair gazing down at her hands folded in her lap. One by one, in silence, the people in the room went up to kneel to her and let her take their heads between her hands and then look into her eyes. The silence she brought with her into the room was unlike any I had ever experienced—deeper, full of uncanny, wounding joy. I found my mind becalmed, unable to grasp at any of the thoughts that were racing through it. I had never knelt to anyone else, and I had never before seen one human being kneel to another, and yet nothing in the worship that I saw before me struck me as blasphemous. Meera seemed to know intimately each head she took into her hands; and her eyes changed for each person who approached her. She did not take the worship offered for herself. There was no self in her; only a Presence like the red-gold sunlight and warm wind that filled the room. To kneel to this girl in this room seemed even familiar. It was like kneeling to the sea wind, or to a sudden vision of snow on the mountains, or to a moment of supreme eloquence in music.

From the beginning the courage of what Meera did moved me. There she sat, a seventeen-year-old girl, surrounded by no ritual paraphernalia, offering neither discourses nor speeches, only her presence, her touch, her gaze. She was unlike anything I had ever imagined as a Master—no white beard or face scored with the world's pain and wisdom. Yet the authority with which she conducted herself was complete.

She was either mad or genuine, and nothing in the atmosphere suggested anything unbalanced.

I knelt to her and for the first time felt the delicate, taut softness of her hands on each side of my head. I had come full of questions, but they all fell from me. As her fingers held my head I saw in my mind's eye the painting by Velázquez in the National Gallery "Mary as Queen of Heaven," where a Spanish woman, grave and soberly dressed, is shown against a stormy night sky ringed by moons and stars. The woman in the painting had changed into Meera. I heard inwardly, "I am the Queen of Heaven," spoken in a lisping child's voice. The words repeated themselves in all the languages I knew—English, French, German, Italian. It was so clear a vision, I had some difficulty when I opened my eyes in readjusting to the room I was in and to the calm and compassionate eyes that were now staring into mine.

Back in my chair I closed my eyes to try to keep the marvel of what had been shown me. On the inside of my eyelids (I can put it no other way) I saw, clearly, and in golden light, Sri Aurobindo's face, still, unsmiling, but very alive. I blinked several times, thinking I was imagining it. The face remained, gazing into me. The vision stayed for nearly ten minutes, refusing to allow me to doubt it.

"How do you feel?" asked Jean-Marc afterward.

"Calm. And shattered."

We walked silently arm in arm by the sea.

"Before this afternoon with her I felt I knew nothing. Now I feel I know less than nothing. Meera is only seventeen. From what I read in the sheaf of papers you gave me this morning she has had no masters herself in this world, done no spiritual discipline. None of this makes sense."

Jean-Marc clapped his hands and laughed.

"If it made any human sense, it would not be what it is."

"And what is it?"

"I don't have the words yet. I am waiting to be shown. So must you. Don't read anything now. Open. Have the courage just to open."

I put my books aside, and spent the next days walking and meditating by Aurobindo's tomb and trying hard not to let fear or doubt ruin the miracle of what had begun. Each evening Jean-Marc and I returned to the small house at the center of town at a quarter to five.

The sense of peace deepened. I became more and more grateful for the luminous silence of that white bare room with its curtains blowing in the breeze, its bowls of always fresh flowers, its light fragrance of incense. Her silence was a blessing. All my life I had worked with words, wanted to use them, to master them; nearly everything I had learned had come to me through words. But in Meera's silence I returned to a deeper learning, the one I experienced in music when my whole being was addressed, the one I had known as a child, sitting reading by my mother as she slept, or playing canasta with her on the beach, watching the sea.

Fears struck at me, and doubts, but always every evening Meera would remove them, simply by being herself, seated in her chair with such simple love. I had no idea who or what she was; I knew only that she was something I had never seen before, and that I was more at home with her than with anyone else.

After one *darshan* Jean-Marc and I were walking away from the house. We had gone about a hundred yards when Jean-

Marc looked back, pulled my sleeve, and pointed. There, alone on the house's tiny balcony, stood Meera in her sari, looking down at us, the dusk sun spilling over her body.

We stood in the street, with our hands folded in prayer, returning her molten gaze, and the bicycles parted around us.

Two days later, on January sixth, Epiphany, Mother Meera ended one idea of reality for me for good. She did something from which my life never recovered.

It was early evening. *Darshan* had been unusually long—two hours. Jean-Marc, I, and an American were standing outside the door of Meera's apartment putting on our shoes.

The door opened with a sharp clack. Still in the brilliant red sari she had worn for *darshan,* stood Meera alone. All around her, as she stood there gazing at us with a passion I had never seen before on her face, was a blaze of Light—white diamond Light—all the brighter for being in the darkness of the doorway. I began to tremble and perspire. The Light streamed from her; her skin was a deep fiery gold; her eyes blazed, vast and abstract, like two bonfires in the darkness. The Light was of the same pure, piercing whiteness that I had seen in the vision Aurobindo had given me the year before. I gazed at it around Meera, hardly able to believe what I was seeing. That it emanated from her and not from any other source was unmistakable; beyond any doubt I was seeing with open eyes the Divine Light and Meera burning in it.

We all three saw the Light, simultaneously, together, and were unable to move or say anything.

Slowly, with profound tenderness, Meera turned to each of us and transformed herself before our eyes. She turned to Jean-Marc and became immediately the Goddess of his inner dream—warm, sensuous, smiling, her head tilted slightly. She turned to the American and seemed to melt, visibly, into another shape—to grow taller, older, to become hieratic, and grave with the majesty I had seen in her when she appeared to my inner eye as the Queen of Heaven. Then she turned to me. Her face seemed to detach itself from her body and swim, burning, back and forth in the air before me. There was nothing but her face. I did not know whether it was separate from me or within me; all sense of distance was obliterated. The Light became more and more intense, so bright that it took all my strength to go on looking into it. The face was smiling—not gently as it had to Jean-Marc but with a tigerish, exultant smile, a smile of absolute triumph. She gazed deep into my eyes; my whole body filled with flame. In the seconds of that gaze I was only my eyes and this Fire.

The three of us had, as if in a dream, raised our hands to salute her. Meera became "herself" again and raptly saluted us each in turn. The humility of this gesture pierced me even more deeply than the glory of the smile she had given me. She was saluting, I realized, the divine Self in each of us. "You, too, are this Light that I am," her gesture told us. "You are Me and I am you and we are inseparable forever."

Then she bowed her head and closed the door quietly.

Jean-Marc and I went out and lay by the sea, unable to speak for long, marvelous hours.

Then he said, "One life is over."

"My life," I said slowly, "will be a choice between the madness of what occurred in the doorway and the madness of the world. I hope I will have the courage—"

Jean-Marc interrupted me. "You will never escape what you saw. Wherever you run, the vision of her standing there burning in Divine Light will follow you. Look at your face!

You've just seen the Divine and you look like a character out of bad Ibsen. I would have thought even *your* love of drama had had enough for one night."

I lay back on the sand.

"I imagined a thousand things for my life but never this . . ." I was stammering comically.

Back in my room by the sea I prayed to Aurobindo for guidance and opened *The Mother* at these words:

> The Mother not only governs all from above
> but she descends into this lesser triple uni-
> verse. . . . She has consented to the great sacri-
> fice and has put on like a mask the soul and
> forms of the Ignorance.

I saw Meera's face as it had been in the doorway, turned toward me. For the first time that evening, as I prayed to her, I found myself using the word *Ma*. I had been shy of calling a girl ten years younger than myself the Indian name for "Mother," but no other name seemed appropriate.

"Ma," I prayed, "I know almost nothing of you. Teach me."

There is a violent beauty in revelation that the soul loves but the ego fears as death. The days after Ma's manifestation of her nature were ones of total turmoil. Every inner resistance I had to Her, to Indian mysticism, to the mystical in general raged inside me, and my analytical mind tried desperately to reclaim my life. In the worst moments I felt that Ma had taken me over, that she had used her powers to stifle and enchain me, her Light to enslave me. The absurdity of these doubts only made me suffer more. How would I ever be free of them? How long would it be before I could accept the simplicity of this new dimension of direct contact with the Divine she was opening to me?

Jean-Marc did the best thing he could have done for me in those days: He laughed. He found my struggles irrepressibly funny. He would say that watching me act out was much, much better than the cinema and it was free.

"This struggle is necessary and it will go on. I went through it, too, at the beginning. You must come to know everything in you that refuses Her. *Everything.* And that will mean a complete unmasking of yourself to yourself."


Two days before I was due to return to America I was still in turmoil. I went to *darshan,* angry, and Ma held my head a long time, as if draining it of darkness. I sat down and again saw Aurobindo's face when I closed my eyes, surrounded by golden Light. Peace, at last, at long last, descended, and I wanted to weep with relief.

Later I walked on the beach with a professor of religious studies from Arizona, who had also been at *darshan.* He kept saying things like "She sure is something, ain't she?" and I wanted to leave him to walk alone. But as soon as I thought that, I felt my mind go silent, as if someone had picked it up, shaken and emptied it. I turned to look at the wizened, squat face of the professor and, instead of the superior distaste I had been indulging, I began to feel affection for him.

I gazed at the sand by the professor's feet as he kept talking, and slowly it began to shine with the same milky light I had seen months ago on the beach in Pondicherry when I had heard the OM of the Brahman. I prayed to Ma inwardly: "Show me your Divine Love."

The professor and I sat on the sand and talked of Plato and the vision of Love in the *Symposium.* He said he found Plato "repressive," a fantasist; that such a Love could not exist; and that a commonsense charity was more valuable than all Socrates' attempts to define a Love beyond time and space. But as he was talking I found myself being filled with just that Love he said did not exist: He, the sand, the moonlight on the sand, my worn, green plastic sandals, the pile of turds about fifty yards away, the sleeping mangy black dog to our left—all became vibrant with milky light, visibly blessed.

I began to speak, and words I had never before used rose from me. I talked of Divine Love and its fullness, a fullness beyond anything the ego can imagine; I found myself speaking of Ma and how in her love for us nothing had been repressed or left out, but each desire had been brought to clear perfection. I understood, as I spoke, that the end of the Yoga, the spiritual discipline, I was beginning with her was not detachment, not any kind of empty and bare nirvana, but an infinite expansion of the heart to include all things and all beings. Ma's own love for me seemed to fill me. I heard for the first time the full voice of my own soul, released by her power, and as I spoke I glimpsed, too, the truth to which all my sexual hunger was essentially directed, the home where it would, one day, with her guidance, find not merely peace but a fulfillment beyond anything physical possession could bring.

The professor from Arizona shook his head slowly. "You sure have the Plato bug bad, but I guess all Britishers do," he said.

I laughed; we parted, and I returned to my room. My body seemed lighter, as if it were hardly there at all. I remember thinking it was a walrus of soft light and had to be handled with care, and I laid it out consciously along my bed.

Then, calmly and strongly, a voice began to speak to me. There was no mistaking this voice; drunk as I was on the power Ma was filling me with, I was at the same time lucid. Over and over, with dazzling variations and images, the voice said: *You cannot transform what you have not blessed. You can never transform what first you have not accepted and blessed.* I realized the voice was telling me to bless and accept my sexual nature, which had filled my youth with loneliness, pain, and guilt. I had to love my sexuality fearlessly before I could transform it; suppression or denial would not work. I could not run to Divine Love without having truly experienced human love and given myself to it: What would I have to offer Ma if my heart and body had not been opened? My understanding of spiritual discipline had been fearful, self-righteous; true discipline, Ma was showing me, would be one entirely in the service of love, of an always deepening and expanding experience of love.

As the voice was speaking I felt Ma's hands on my head. I realized, with great joy, that Ma was freeing me from every guilt, every shame. She did not want a puritanical disciple; she wanted one who was mature, who had opened to every form of love and understood, through suffering if necessary, its true place. My temperament could only grow in freedom, a freedom that might entail danger and mistakes; I knew that now and knew that she knew it and blessed it. I could not sleep all night for happiness and relief.

The next evening's *darshan* was the final one of that visit. Afterward I sat with Ma's guardian, Mr. Reddy. His constant gentleness and solicitousness had made me want to talk to him truthfully before I left, and I told him what I had experienced the evening before.

"You are still a very young man." He smiled, taking my hands in his. "You must live your life. In India we say you must become *pakka*."

I remembered the word from my childhood. "It means correct, doesn't it?"

"That is one of its meanings. Its deepest meaning is ripe. You must become ripe. Ma will ripen you and give you all the experiences, good and bad, that you need to come to your completeness." And then he looked at me mischievously. "And then she will put up her hand and pluck you off the tree."

"And then?"

"Oh, then," he said, closing his eyes, "then everything real begins. Because then you are eaten, and by Her."

Ma came and stood in the doorway. Mr. Reddy looked at her and whispered, "To be eaten completely by the Divine is to become immortal."

Ma stood looking at us looking at her and then lowered her head, smiling, as if to herself.

A silence full of power filled the room.

"Of course," said Mr. Reddy, smiling, "to be eaten by God, you have to be very, very tasty."

"And how do you become tasty?"

He took his hands away from mine and folded them.

"By suffering, and love, and prayer, and humble longing."

Ma said something in telugu—the first time I had heard her speak. Her voice was soft and very low, almost inaudible.

"Ma said whatever happens you are never to be afraid. You are her Child. The Grace is with you."

I looked up at her and said, "Help me to understand."

She nodded.

Ma went into the other room and returned with a plate with an orange on it. She came to me and held out the plate.

"You see," said Mr. Reddy, "you must eat the orange the Mother is offering you."

I took the orange. Ma broke into a quiet laugh.

"Don't just hold it," Mr. Reddy said, "eat it."


ॐ I returned to Cornell. Months of gloom and bewilderment followed. None of my friends could follow what I was attempting to express to them, partly because my understanding was still so fragmented. Many of them thought I was on the verge of a breakdown. The story of meeting a seventeen-year-old girl who was the Divine Mother and who had appeared in a doorway in Divine Light etc., etc., struck them as not only ludicrous but dangerous. In April I gave a lecture at the university on Aurobindo; I poured all I had lived into it. One famous literary critic got up at the end and asked, "Is Mr. Harvey seriously suggesting that we save the world by yogic meditation on our navel?" Another famous anthropologist said he thought there were some nice parallels between what Aurobindo was saying and early Derrida.

A war began in my psyche that was to drag on for many years. Everything I had learned and aspired to in my career as academic and writer struggled against Her. I wanted acceptance from a world I despised, success in a way I disapproved of, approbation from just those people whom I knew to be narrow and corrupt. A life unsupported and alone, dedicated entirely to the pursuit of spiritual awakening, seemed impossible to sustain.

It was during this time that the most painful of my love affairs began with someone younger than myself, C, who would eventually go mad. Our relationship was sexually problematic from the beginning, and my despair at not being able to consumate the tenderness I felt sickened my life. I could not work truly in the West or completely retire to the East, nor could I love or be loved without horror. Ma showed me in dreams and meditation that I had to go on loving, even though I knew I would only be torn apart. I did not completely understand why I *had to* consent to torment without fear or self-protection, but I continued.

I returned to Pondicherry in May 1978, in a great deal of pain. I had imagined, I suppose, that meeting Ma that winter would settle my life. Instead, it drove me into a passion of confusion I had never before known. The effort to bless my sexuality as the vision had told me led me to a love that was the deepest and most agonizing of my life; again and again I found I had to bless despair, not the flowering of delight and self-acceptance I had longed for.

I hoped, on returning to Pondicherry that May, that being with Ma and seeing her every day would shift something. Day after day I would go to *darshan*, expecting a miracle and receiving, as I thought, nothing, neither the silence I had known before nor the peace I longed for. I never doubted Her; I doubted myself. I doubted whether I could ever be brave or lucid or skilled enough to feel what she was, to enter through the door I knew she had opened for me. My own inexpertness appalled me; I felt self-obsessed and full of unfocused hunger; I began to realize how helpless the ego is before the Divine, but the knowledge of this helplessness did not make me humble—it made me afraid. What would I have without my ego? That old formation of thoughts and habit I called myself was in pain, but it was all I had. What else could I rely on? I had glimpsed the soul only on rare occasions; how could I call on its continual presence? The only way to establish a lasting contact with it would be through a spiritual discipline; I prayed and meditated, read and contemplated the great mystical texts of the world, but nothing brought me closer to abandon or fearlessness. I began to feel I would be blocked always, waiting always like the man in Kafka's parable, by a door that would never open. The prospect of staying before it forever was worse even than the emotional suffering I was enduring.

Jean-Marc was undergoing difficulties of his own. "I feel sometimes," he said, "as if I have no head. And at other times bliss shakes my whole being." His greater experience and more patient nature, however, made him accept more readily than I did what he could not yet understand.

"I know all this is Grace," he would say. "I know, too, that one day I will understand it. But, *mon Dieu*, it is not always a joke to be in the paws of the Lion."

ॐ "Look at us." Jean-Marc laughed as we walked by the sea. "Two clowns in the circus of the Mother. I feel like such a clown. And it isn't always such a bad feeling. But for you, who likes grander roles, it must be terrible."

"I hate being ridiculous, and every day I feel more so."

"Good," said Jean-Marc. "I, too, feel almost completely . . ." he carefully sought the word, "irrelevant. Yes, that is it—the old self is now completely *irrelevant*."

"But still there."

"Still there, and in many ways hungrier and more insistent than ever. Comic, no?"

"Only partly," I said, wincing.

"One day they will seem wholly comic, all these months or years of bleeding, analyzing, suffering. Wholly comic."

We sat down by the edge of the sea and let it wash all over us.

"Each day I love Her more," Jean-Marc said. "I see the gap between us more and more, and yet I feel her tenderness for me more and more deeply. Like everything else in this experience, that is paradoxical. How can She be so far and yet so close, the closest thing, closer even than this sand I'm rubbing through my fingers?"

"What do you think clarity about all this will be like?"

"Lightning," he said. "Lightning that illuminates a whole landscape and makes you want to laugh wildly."

Three days later I was in Mahabalipuram and saw that lightning.

I was walking on the beach when, out of nowhere, a storm began. I had not consciously noticed any clouds before, or even a darkening of the brash sunlight. Yet abruptly, all around me, across the whole space of the sky, lightning began to play.

A torrential rain began, lashing me from all sides. I panicked, ran to hide under some bushes, and sat there, cowering.

Suddenly I heard a voice: *Get out onto the sand. Take your clothes off. Dance.*

The rain was beating the bush under which I crouched. Suddenly the idea of trying to keep dry seemed ludicrous. I stripped off my clothes and ran naked into the sea.

At that moment a vast thunderclap shook the horizon, and lightning shattered the bushes under which I had been hiding.

Laughter seized me and made me dance wildly around and around in the rain and lightning until I fell, still laughing, wet and naked onto the sand.

At that moment I saw Ma's face in the air before me wearing the same exultant smile it had on the night she had appeared in the doorway.

*Why do you doubt me? Why do you cling to safeties that do not last? Why do you fear even the most terrible storm when I am always with you?*


That night, half out of my mind, I sat in the Shore Temple as the sun went down.

An old woman was worshipping the lingam, singing, thinking she was alone, all the names of Shiva. She wore a tattered blue sari, and her face was scarred by hunger and loneliness. As she sang the sea grew wilder and crept up the shore until it broke over the lingam. She sang louder at every wave that thrashed her.

Something in my heart broke open as I watched her. I was being given an image of what true love of the Divine is, an image that shamed my rebellion and selfish misery.

The old woman started to dance around the lingam, but the sea felled her and she collapsed with her arms around the symbol of God, her eyes closed, still singing.

ॐ The next day, June ninth, was my twenty-seventh birth-day. I returned to Pondicherry for Mother's *darshan*.

After *darshan* the devotees were told to stay. Mother had cooked food and was going to serve it to us. How could the Force that had appeared in Mahabalipuram be the same as this simple Indian girl dressed in a blue sari, coming through the door with rice and curry, placing plates by each of us and slowly, delicately, filling them? We could not take our eyes off her, not just because of her beauty, but because of the grace in her every gesture—the way she poured the water, the way she arranged the food on the plate, the way she walked, flowingly, like a young dancer. We ate in silence and tasted each mouthful; she watched us from the doorway, with the evening sunlight playing in her hair.

She can be anything she wants, I realized. She can be the storm and the Face in the storm; she can be the Master, replying simply to the most difficult questions; she can be the majestic Being at *darshan*, pouring her soul in silence into ours; she can be this young girl in the doorway, smiling as we ate her food. She is entirely free to do whatever is necessary to break open our hearts.

After we had finished eating, Jean-Marc said to Ma, "Andrew will sing for you. He has a good voice." He elbowed me in the ribs. "Now you have to."

Ma sat on the small throne and bowed her head. For a moment I had no idea what to sing, but then a medieval carol to the Virgin came to me; I had not sung it since I was ten or eleven.

I sing of a maiden
That is makeless
King of all kings
To her son she ches. . . .

I sang a little shakily, and the room filled with the final gold light of the setting sun.

Ma listened to it with her head bowed and nodded, once, slowly, when it ended.

The sea of gold light around her deepened, and we sat with her, watching the same light that was covering her cover us—every part of our bodies, hands, feet, faces. At the moment the sun began at last to withdraw, Ma smiled and rose.


Afterward Jean-Marc and I wandered by the moonlit sea.

"I don't care who knows it." He laughed. "I am not in my right mind. There is a bliss that breaks from her Presence. It is like a . . ."—he struggled—"it is like a wind."

"Can you imagine me back in Oxford trying to say there is a bliss that breaks from her . . . ?"

We collapsed on the sand in laughter.

"Oh, God, I am so happy," he said. "I don't care what anyone thinks. You're going soon. Keep this happiness alive in you; it is the truth."

I started to smile.

"Why are you smiling?"

"I was imagining trying to define *bliss* in the common room of my college. One of my colleagues, a philosopher, told me the Buddha would have reconsidered enlightenment if he could have heard Mozart's *The Marriage of Figaro*."

Jean-Marc rolled on the sand.

After a moment he took my hands.

"Talk about Her as little as possible. Don't allow anything to shake the experience while it is still young. You are still not strong enough to face the full incomprehension of your world. It's not your nature to keep anything hidden, but be wise this time and *shut up*."

"It will be hard not to say anything."

"If you say anything now, people will think you are mad.

And being away from her and from this astounding atmosphere she is, you might come to believe them. And then everything would start to come undone."

He paused. "I have the feeling what she wants for us all will unravel slowly! Have you seen how Ma walks? One foot carefully placed after the other. She is in no hurry; she has all the time in eternity. Good joke, no?"

"Good joke," I said. "In a week's time I will be back in my rooms in Oxford. Everything will seem a dream."

"This is not a dream . . ."—Jean-Marc pointed to his heart—"the joy that is dancing here, that is dancing between us and in both of us. Never forget this."

He smiled. "The ego forgets everything. It has to, to go on surviving in its dreary theater. But the soul remembers. And one day that memory becomes one continuous fire of bliss and the theater burns down."

In the last days I fell sick from tension and fear of what lay ahead. I had no desire to return to the West, and yet I had to. First to Oxford and then to Upstate New York where Hobart and William Smith Colleges had given me a teaching job for a year. I knew how young I still was in the experience and how vulnerable to scorn. I could see only too well how my experience with her could appear to others: I had lost a mother as a child, and now, with suspicious completeness, found another one who would never abandon me and on whom I could project any magical fantasy I wished because she was remote and silent and herself engaged in a fantasy that matched mine. That this interpretation was absurd didn't stop it from being powerful; its cold voice tormented me.

I grew so ill I couldn't leave my room. Days went by in fever until one afternoon I had another powerful experience I could not doubt. I was not asleep; I had just put down a book

I was desultorily trying to read. I closed my eyes momentarily and was seized by a wind. I opened my eyes; I was not in my room at all but being whirled, like a piece of paper, down a long tunnel and then across what resembled an empty gray desert. I was so terrified, I fainted. I came to standing in a large stinking sewer. All around me lay the bodies of dead rats and other animals, and the stench of the sewer was frightful. I had never experienced fear like the fear of that moment—total, naked, burning up my whole body and mind. I started to scream, but no sound came. I realized I was alone. Around me, in the stinking sewage, crocodiles were moving. I could see them now, hundreds of them in the half light stretching down into the distance.

I felt on the edge of madness. Then I heard a laugh.

Ma was standing in the filth with me, by the wall ten feet to my right, in a green-and-gold sari. I knew it was she though she had the face of a friend at Oxford. "She" was wearing the ring Ma wears on her right hand—a small pearl ring.

The crocodiles came to her, and as she stood, gazing at me, they parted around her, crawling away from me up the walls. I wanted to sob with joy, to run and embrace her. She held up her hand as if to stop me, motioning me instead to close my eyes and then open them. When I did, I was kneeling before her in her room, as if at *darshan*, with the peaceful noises of Pondicherry filtering through the window. I wore gold cotton clothes I had made for my birthday. She took my head into her hands and I returned to my bed in the guest house, still feeling the touch of her hands on my temples.

Three hours later the fever left me.

I went to *darshan*, reeling, unable to speak. In the experience of the afternoon I had been entirely conscious. Nothing, even the gifts of experiences she had already given me, had begun to prepare me for this outrageous breaking of every convention of space and time. How could it ever be understood?

After *darshan* I told Mr. Reddy about what had happened.

He went into the room where Ma was and recounted every-thing. I heard her laugh softly, in exactly the way she had in the vision.

Mr. Reddy came out, smiling broadly, with an apple.

"Ma says she wore the face of your friend because she wants you to know always that she is your friend."

Mr. Reddy gave me the apple.

He held me around the shoulders.

"It takes us all a long, long time before we really understand just how much love she has, and how she will go to any length to show it."

Ma came and stood in the doorway.

Mr. Reddy stretched out his hands to her and said, "Oh, Ma, we are all such fools, and you still give us everything."

Ma pointed to the apple I was holding in my hand.

I ate it in front of her. When I had finished, she came with a plate, took the core, and walked with it into the kitchen.


🕉 I returned to Oxford. The summer darkened into night-mare. My friend C visited from Cornell, and his insta-bility became madness. Witnessing the death of our love brought me near to madness myself, but I had to keep as sane as I could to be of help. Why had this happened after so much beauty in India, so much revelation? I had no idea then. All I could do was pray C would not commit suicide.

C went back to America for treatment. I went to America in late August to take up my position at Hobart and William Smith Colleges in Upstate New York. I still understood very little of the suffering that was consuming me, but I went on teaching and prayed to Ma for clarity and peace. In September, just before Ma, along with Mr. Reddy and Adilakshmi, was to come to the West for the first time (to Montreal, a few hundred miles from where I was), I had a dream.

In it I was living by the sea in a town like Mahabalipuram. I saw myself as a boy sitting on the steps of a temple, singing, dressed in white. As I watched myself the face changed, and many different faces passed across it—all Indian, some old, some childlike, some adolescent. Then I heard a voice say, *In only a few years you will see the sea. Have no fear. You will see the sea.* I woke up, bathed in quiet. For a few minutes I could not understand the meaning of what had been said. Then I heard again: *The Sea is the sea of Light that all the mystics describe—Shunyata to the Tibetans, Brahman to the Hindus, the Face of Glory, or Sea, to the Sufis.* The voice repeated, *Do not be afraid, whatever terrors now begin. You will see the sea.* I looked up at the ceiling of my bedroom; it had started to pulsate, as if melting in invisible fire.

In a meditation two days later I heard the same voice say, *You cannot understand what is happening now. But you will understand. Trust her.*

"I am not strong enough to trust her," I said.

*Don't worry.* The voice laughed. *Even then she will save you.*

Ma arrived in Montreal in September 1979. I went to see her in late October. On the bus to Montreal I read this in Rolle's *Fire of Love*: "This is what the perfect lover does: He completely strips himself for the sake of the one he loves, nor will he allow himself to be clothed in anything except in that which he loves."

The words wounded me. I was so far from any real self-abandon to Her, and I knew that something in me would never be content until I was ready to give her everything.

In Montreal Mr. Reddy told me, "A great Master is like a skilled fisherman: he doesn't pull the fish in at once, kicking and pulling against him. He reels it in slowly, exhausting its resistance on the way."

Then he said, "Don't worry. You will see the Great Sea."
I started. I had not told him my dream.

*In a notebook of that visit I wrote:*

Ma herself has never seemed more serene. "Plans" and "visions" seethe around her, but she is free and alone. She gives *darshan* now sometimes to three hundred people in a large, soulless auditorium, sitting alone on the stage, looking at everyone in turn. How can it be that all feel seen by her? And yet they do.

She is giving me, I saw tonight, what I need—a deepened experience of meditation. Just after she looked at me, it happened. My body fell away into a peace that felt like snow—immense, still coolness.

D afterward: "But what exactly is her teaching?"

Mr. Reddy: "Union in silence with all Being and action flowing from that Silence in enlightened joy."

D: "That isn't a teaching."

Mr. Reddy: "No, it is a revolution. More interesting, no?"

D: "How does this revolution *work*?"

Mr. Reddy: "Why does everyone want teaching and no one want *experience*? What the soul wants is ecstasy and knowledge; the Mother gives both. Why don't you just sit down, be quiet, and *receive*? I know why. To listen to teaching is much more easy. Then you can feel clever. You cannot feel clever sitting and receiving. You have to be a *little* humble, no? That is hard. Andrew likes to talk and be clever, but even he is learning how to shut up." His face broke into a wide grin. "Slowly."

D: "How do we *learn* to receive?"

Mr. Reddy laughed his rich, deep Indian laugh. "In the West everyone has to *learn* everything. There has to be a manual. Do this, then do that, then stand on your head, then breathe in and out." He wiped his eyes. "My dear sir, just look at Ma. Doesn't some sort of love spring up in your heart? Well then, follow that love, however small it is. It will take you to a fountain. All you have to do then is sit in the fountain and get cool."

D: "All this is very *Indian*."

"No," said Mr. Reddy, "it is not Indian, or Chinese, or American. It is natural. It is simple. Ma is simple and God is simple and love is simple and receiving is simple."

Ma came into the room with a bowl of fresh flowers. Her entry was so silent, we hardly knew she was there until she stood before us. No one could say anything.

Mr. Reddy gazed at her. Tears stood, calm and shining, in his eyes.

The next afternoon I went on a walk alone with Mr. Reddy, who looked regal in a smart dark suit and black coat. Snow had just fallen on the streets of Montreal. We had to walk slowly and gingerly, holding onto each other to keep from falling.

Mr. Reddy's compassion made it possible to talk with him about anything, and I spoke of C's madness, and my anguish.

"Go on loving your friend, whatever happens," he said. "Learn through this to love without expecting anything. To love the Divine you must be prepared to give everything and ask nothing. With C you can train for this abandon. The heart must break to become *large*. When the heart is broken open, then God can put the whole universe in it."

He spoke with such fervor, I realized he was speaking from his own experience.

Mr. Reddy stopped in the snow.

"Let me tell you something. Meeting Ma and beginning to see who she is has put you in the field of an immense Force.

That Force will lead you to the truth. Ma uses the whole of life as her instruction. During the next years you will find that into your life will come all those necessary to teach you and lead you forward. Ma teaches everyone in his or her own way, in terms of each one's stage of development and temperament and past. Ma will complete you; she will bring you to a deep knowledge of yourself. Then you will be ready to go on the journey with her. When you have begun that journey, the whole pattern of her work in your life will be revealed and you will laugh with her at the precision and mercy of it. What looks like agony now is leading to a joy vaster than you can imagine. What looks like humiliation will guide you to humility."

He held my shoulder. "Remember when I talked to you about the word *pakka* in Pondicherry? Everything that will now happen to you will be designed to ripen you. To be of use to Ma, you must know everything about your own nature; to do her work, you must have truly understood the world, not fled from it. Ma wants people to be juicy."

I laughed. "Juicy?"

"Yes, full of passion and humor, truly human."

He walked on, shaking the snow from his boots.

"Some great souls arrive here already purified. The rest have to learn the hollowness of the world and the pain of desire. You will have to learn. Ma will teach you fast, if you let her. And something in you will. Because you want enlightenment."

He said the last sentence looking at me very gravely.

"Are you sure?"

"I am certain. Something in you will go through anything to become wise."

"How do you know?"

"Behind your facile cleverness and worldliness is a Child, a Divine Child. I see his face distinctly. He will take the rest of you through *anything* to get you to Her. And he will succeed."

"And then?"

"Then you will become Him. It is simple."

"It doesn't seem simple."

"To the ego *nothing* seems simple. To the soul everything *always* is."

ॐ During the next months, back in Upstate New York, I remembered Mr. Reddy's advice. My grief over C deepened—but with that deepening came acceptance. I refused to try to stop loving C; I tried not to demand anything or expect anything and to wish only his recovery. The reward came in the feeling toward him of a free tenderness, wider and more absolute than anything I had known.

One night I dreamed that C and I came into a room where Ma was. She was dressed in a red-and-gold sari and stood by the window. She took C into her arms, and he began to sob. Then she turned to me and told me to take off my shirt. I took it off, and she placed a hand on my chest. Immediately, throughout my body, shot a sensation of anguishing sweet fire. I felt my heart expand and throb so wildly, I thought my chest would break open. Then I awoke and heard the voice: *C is the spear through which I have opened your heart. Now it can never close.*

Lying in the dark, I realized that what had been wrong in my love for C had been my attempt to confine the great love I felt only to him; what C had helped to awaken in me was a love that could embrace everything. It was not the love for C that was wrong but rather its exclusiveness, its idolatry, its confusion of C with the radiance that was shining through him. It was toward the source of that radiance—divine beauty and divine love—that I had now to point my life.

Mr. Reddy had said in Montreal: "During the next years you will find that into your life will come all those necessary to teach you and lead you forward."

The summer of 1980 found me in Ladakh, a part of old Tibet that is now in India. I was guided there to one of the greatest Tibetan masters then living, Thuksey Rinpoche, with whom I fell spiritually in love and whose impact on my inner life has been second only to Ma's own.

I have written my love for Thuksey Rinpoche and the revelations his wisdom brought in my book *A Journey in Ladakh*. In that book I made no mention of Ma; she was still too profound a mystery for me to begin to speak of her. But as my relationship with the great and golden man who was to be my soul's Father unfolded that summer in the mountains, I knew, from the beginning, that it was a gift Ma was giving me.


When I met the Rinpoche I felt no incompatibility between being Ma's disciple and diving into Tibetan Buddhism. Spiritual love, the profound and unforgettable emotion that shakes the heart in the presence of holiness, is one of the most direct of all human feelings and the most difficult to explain or deny. I knew from the first moment I saw the Rinpoche seated in the half dark of a shrine room in Shey monastery surrounded by butter lamps and quietly chanting monks that I had been intended to meet him. His majesty—he was a strongly built, beautiful man in his early sixties with a leonine head—and the atmosphere of charged and ringing silence refreshed me as soon as I entered it. One of his monks, an Australian who had left a banking career to follow him into the mountains, described him as "a calm bonfire of wisdom and love that nothing can put out." Over several weeks in the mountains I sat near that bonfire and warmed my being by its glow.

I returned briefly from Shey to Leh, the capital city of Ladakh, a little stunned at the rapidity and wildness with which everything had happened, but certain of its justice. There I was given a clear image of the Rinpoche's and Mother's relationship.

It was the end of August: Krishna's birthday was being celebrated in Leh. A rickety float laden with flowers was being slowly, laboriously dragged up the main street. I went out of the small *samosa* shop where I was eating lunch to watch it. On the float, giggling and looking coy, were two children: a boy, dressed in purple and yellow and heavily made-up as Krishna, and a girl, slightly larger and sulky-looking in the most garish pink, green, and red sari as Radha, his cosmic beloved and one of the manifestations of the Mother in Hinduism.

As I watched, all sound ceased. I could not hear anything although I could still see, with increasingly hallucinatory precision, everything around me—the faces of the bored Sikh soldiers in the crowd, the Ladakhi women bending over the baskets of vegetables by the side of the road, the wilting marigolds hung in clumps from the side of the float. I looked up at the boy Krishna and saw, clearly, the face of the Rinpoche. I looked across at Radha and saw, with equal clarity, Ma's face. What happened then I do not remember. Sometime later I found myself flat out on my bed in the small glass room I rented, my hearing restored, with a thunderstorm raging around me.

My whole room seemed to shake and crackle in the storm, and I found myself laughing with the same wildness as on the beach in Mahabalipuram. Each roll of thunder said distinctly, with a vast booming voice, *This is it. This is it. This is it. This is it.*

This moment is liberation, is reality. Nothing but this. Now.

I gazed out of the window, howling, now, half in pain, half in an ecstasy more uncontrollable than any other I had been given. The mountains were transparent as if made of rice paper. I saw through them valleys, other mountains, the plains of India, cities . . . receding, receding into the distance.

I do not remember what happened next. I seemed to fall asleep again. I awoke, hours later, to an almost full moon staring at me through my open window.

My father had been mostly absent in my life; in the Rinpoche I found at last a man whom I could revere. In him I experienced what an illumined male could be like, how kingly and expansive, how able to encompass all the ranges of feeling without fear. The Rinpoche could be Mother as well as Father, Child as well as Sage. I saw in him the human completeness I longed for, and began to believe, because of his example, that I, too, could one day attain it. I had always disliked the strain of escapism found in a good deal of mysticism and discovered in Tibetan Buddhism an ideal of an enlightenment spent in unremitting service to others that reconciled the claims of the Divine and those of ordinary life. In Thuksey Rinpoche I saw that ideal lived out and understood, and through him, that the mystic quest was of supreme importance not just in itself but also for the healing powers it gave the person who successfully completed it to pour back into the world. I needed assurance that the quest was not another, more esoteric form of egoism; the Rinpoche gave it to me.

In learning to love him, I prepared myself to love Ma more completely. Sacred love, like any other, has to be practiced; in opening my heart to an intimate and holy devotion to him, he prepared me for the journey I would take with her years later.

In the Isha Upanishad it is written: "The Face of Truth is

covered with a brilliant golden lid." The Rinpoche was that brilliant golden lid for me—the concentrated light of truth in a human being—Ma the Face of Truth behind him. Training my eyes in his radiance made me eventually strong enough to face the blaze of her face behind him.

ॐ I stayed in Ladakh two months. Then the Rinpoche returned to his monastery in Darjeeling. I decided to spend the last month of my vacation in Pondicherry with Ma. When I arrived in Pondicherry, I found that Ma, with Adilakshmi and Mr. Reddy, had gone to Kakinada, a town I had never heard of, in Andhra Pradesh. Mr. Reddy had had to go to a naturopath clinic for dental treatment. I decided to follow them.

The night before I left Pondicherry I had a dream in which I stumbled through a landscape of blinding white sand to a wooden hut. I opened the door of the hut to find Ma standing alone in it.

On a table there was prepared food.

"For you," Ma said. "Sit down."

# THREE

Only Meera, I thought, dragging my decaying baggage from the train at the Kakinada station; "only Meera could have brought me to this place." Kakinada that summer, and I imagine any summer, was hot and filthy—a commercial shantytown with garish rickety pink-and-green buildings and streets chocked with rain-soaked cow dung. I stayed in a hotel called the Venus Lodge, perhaps the worst of all the many bad hotels I have known in India. In it I reread Aurobindo's *The Synthesis of Yoga* while fat executives shouted and sang songs drunkenly and smashed bottles against walls. The manager of the hotel, a bald hunchback with seven gold teeth who never changed his dhoti, kept asking me, "Why, dearest sir, are you here?" I would always reply, "To see a young girl who is the Mother, the Shakti." He would shake his head.

"Very good joke, sir. English very funny people."

Ma, Mr. Reddy, and Adilakshmi lived alone in a large, roomy white house about a mile from the hotel, lent to them by one of Ma's Indian devotees.

"You are lucky," Mr. Reddy said when he first saw me, clasping my hands. "Now you will have us all to yourself. We can meet every day and talk of nothing but her. I will tell you everything I know." He smiled. "Well, not *everything*. Some things can only be learned gradually; otherwise your head would explode." He found this very funny. "And then what would I say to your Oxford college? Mr. Harvey's head has exploded. I would be put in jail, no?"

I quoted to him from an Emily Dickinson poem: "The truth must dazzle gradually . . . or all the world be blind."

"Ah," he said, "she was a wise woman."

ॐ I saw very little of Ma in the first few days. Each morning I would walk across Kakinada, past the beggars picking lice out of their hair, past the blaring radios of the tea shops and the open sewers, to the oasis of sun-washed silence where she lived.

Sometimes I would catch sight of her sewing at a window; sometimes she would smile to me as she came in from shopping with Adilakshmi—a rapid shy smile, lowering her head; sometimes I would be talking with Mr. Reddy and she would come in for a moment, with a hot saucepan, or a basket full of fresh beans, and stand by the door. As the days went on the sense of her presence grew stronger; I grew to feel a wall of silent light around the house and that every morning I was entering a different world, one that had, as if from a kind of tact, elements of the old world—the creaking white sofa, the chairs with gently rotting canes, the white cups, the red-and-green curtains bodying the wind—but was really another dimension altogether.

Mr. Reddy abetted this feeling. Always neat in his white dhoti, sick but gleaning with love for Ma, he would greet me every morning with joy and we would converse for hours. His talk was always ecstatic and soaked with love of her. He existed in and for Ma. Almost every day he would quote this passage from the Gita to me about his love for her: "You are my mother, father, brother, sister, and everything to me. Without you there is nothing. I cannot exist without you," and the tears would fill his large, somber eyes and he would be unable to continue. I remember the first day I was there, sitting with him in one of the outside rooms. Ma came in. Mr. Reddy looked up and said very softly, "Ma has come," as if announcing a miracle.

I have never known anyone to love another person as Mr. Reddy loved Ma. His love had long ago lost all worldly protections or coverings; it was as free, as transparent, as the love of a child. The fact that he was in his middle fifties and she only eighteen made this extremely mysterious. Whenever I read the end of *King Lear* and think of the love that Lear and Cordelia would have known had Cordelia lived, I think of Ma and Mr. Reddy in those weeks in Kakinada—perfectly happy, living in almost ringing silence, in a rambling old white house.

"You are like a child with Ma," I said to Mr. Reddy.

"And she is like a child with me, no? And then sometimes she is very, very old like a grandmother. And sometimes like a sister. Love has many masks and shapes."

He paused. "I have surrendered everything to her, you see. I live only for her. Have you seen a fisherman bring up his nets? The fish struggle and thresh, cutting themselves to pieces on the ropes. In the end we must learn to lie quietly, to surrender everything."

I saw the beaches of my childhood as he spoke, the fishermen in their ancient wooden catamarans, the silver flash of the piles of fish on the sand.

"I am a great big white fish," he said, "lying in the net of the Mother. Some people might think looking at my life: Ah, he gave up everything for her. In one way I have. I have left my family; I have left the ashram in Pondicherry where I spent twenty years; I have left my only daughter whom I loved. I have left my lands and my world and my money. I have nothing now, nothing but her. But in being with her, I have everything."

There was a silence. "Tell me how you met her," I requested.

He beamed. He never tired of telling of his love for her. He told it simply as if it were a great ancient story, something out of the Ramayana or Mahabharata, something timeless that had only incidentally happened to him.

"I looked for the Mother a long, long time before I found her," he began slowly. "For as long as I can remember, since my earliest childhood, I was looking for Her. I loved my own mother, but I was looking for another one. I used to cry for months together for this "mother." No one understood why. When I was very young, I read a book about Sarada Devi, the wife of Ramakrishna. I wept. I still weep when I read that book. In dreams I used to see the face of a young girl with large dark eyes—*that* was the Mother I was looking for, I knew. But how to find her?"

He gazed intensely at the wall in front of him as if seeing those eyes again.

"All my youth I was hungry and restless. Up to 1950 I did special service with the great Gandhian politician Vinoba Bhave, helping with his land reform. It was not my right work, even though it was good. I grew exhausted and wanted to be free. I did not want God. I just wanted to be free and was desperate to breathe."

His hands gripped the white cane chair, and he closed his eyes.

"The years that followed were bad. I was in pain. I didn't want to work or eat or meet people. I didn't want to sleep— I couldn't sleep. Three times I thought I would kill myself. For hours on end I would feel nothing, think nothing. Doctors said if I went on like that I would go mad. Sometimes I felt mad."

He opened his eyes and looked directly at me.

"I was being purified by pain, set free from all attachment—from family, ambition, money, women. I was being emptied so I could be filled." A crow squawked loudly from the garden.

"At this time," he went on, "I heard of a great female saint called Mannikyamma, who lived near my home near Hyderabad. She was the first of the Mothers I was to live with.

"Mannikyamma had left home at eight years old, refused to marry, run away to a forest where a poor man had found her and helped her by making her a cave in a nearby hill. She stayed there for the rest of her life and was famous for living without food or water. As soon as I heard her name, I had to see her. I climbed up the hill where she was; she greeted me in silence. We meditated for twelve hours without a break.

"Mannikyamma asked me to stay with her. But I knew she was not the Mother I was looking for. That was my intuition. I am a man who has lived his whole life by intuition. Soon after leaving Mannikyamma I heard of another female saint, Chinnama. A friend told me about this female ascetic who lived without clothes. If she tried to put on clothes, she said, they burned away on her body. She was the naked Self so must go naked. Chinnama's belief was that everything should come of itself. She lived abandoned to the will of God and lived on what people brought her to eat.

"I went to see Chinnama and immediately loved her. I felt that by being with her, by being in her presence, I understood all the scriptures. I shall never forget the first moment I saw her. I knew I had come into the presence of a Mother. All thought of the world, of a job or family or fortune, vanished from me when I was near her. I believed I wanted nothing more than to spend the rest of my life at her feet. I gave up my work with Bhave and meditated with Chinnama for four years. My family was angry. There I was, a young man, staying with an Avadhuta, a realized being, in a hut, not working, not being in family life. I wasn't studying with Chinnama either. I didn't feel any need to. Just living and being with her was enough. Even the Gita seemed nothing to what I understood with her.

"At the end of the four years Chinnama told me that only the company of Adiparashakti herself—of the Supreme Divine Mother—would satisfy my soul. I was sad; I loved her so much. Where would I find this Supreme Divine Mother? How would I live without Chinnama?

"I went to a conference in Madras to speak about Chinnama. I met there a man from Pondicherry, a professor. He spoke to me about the yoga of Sri Aurobindo and the great work of transformation being done by Sweet Mother. He invited me to go down to Pondy and see for myself. I stayed three days. When I came back to my village near Hyderabad with Sweet Mother's albums of photographs, my daughter, who was three years old, pointed to one of the photos and said, "I will live with that Mother." I took this as a sign. Soon after I went with my wife and child to Pondy. And there I met the third of the Mothers who have ruled my life. Sweet Mother accepted me into the Pondicherry ashram in 1956."

He paused, looking at his hands. "How happy I was in the ashram! I stayed there between 1956 and 1972. Sweet Mother was very loving and powerful.

"In 1972 I went back to my village to manage my property after my uncle's death. It was then that I first met Kamala Reddy, Mother Meera, who was a ten-year-old girl living in my house." He smiled a beautiful childlike smile. "I had wandered all over India, and I found what I had been looking for in my own home. It is a beautiful divine joke, no? Kamala had the same face as the girl in my dreams."

We sat in a long silence I did not dare break.

"You know," he began again quietly, "I sit here telling you this story, and I still hardly believe it happened to me. But it did. You see it did. I am here, no, telling it to you?"

He pinched himself playfully. "It is a mad story, no?"

At that moment Ma came in wearing a soft green sari with tea for us both. Mr Reddy said something to Ma in telugu, and she replied and left.

"What did you say?"

"I said I had come to the part in the story when she enters and look!—she entered."

"What did she say?"

"That is natural."

The crow from the garden squawked louder this time.

Mr. Reddy smiled. "I am remembering the first time I really experienced Ma's power. It was so beautiful, so funny. Ma had gone to stay fifty miles away. I was lying on my cot one evening. I heard her low, soft voice calling me, and I was amazed. How could she come all that way? I got up and looked for her. She went on calling me. I could not find her anywhere. Later I went to where she was. She said, 'I came to you, and you did not notice anything. I called out to you, and you did not hear.' I asked her how she had come to me. She said, with her mischievous smile, 'There is another way of traveling. Don't you know?' " His smile deepened into laughter. " 'There is another way of traveling. Don't you know?' " he repeated several times, imitating Ma's voice. His hilarity was infectious. I found myself laughing also.

"Many experiences of her power followed the one I told you," he went on, wiping his eyes. "I came to know who she is. I devoted myself to looking after her. I realized I had found the purpose of my life. Ma comes from a loving but poor family. People had always felt she was somehow special—her uncle always used to stop anyone scolding her by saying 'She is not like us. She is different.' But I *knew* who she was. And because she knew I knew she could tell me everything. All her experiences on the higher planes. She could trust me. She knew I believed her; she knew I would do everything I could to help, protect, and prepare her."

He smiled, tilting his head. "Sometimes she would wake

me in the middle of the night to tell me where she had been and what she had been doing. She would sit at the end of my bed and tell me everything—what the gods had said to her, what lessons she had learned, what amazing and beautiful sights she had seen. And so simply, with such childlike grace and wonder. Those were the happiest moments of my life."

For a long moment Mr. Reddy was too moved to go on. Then he whispered, as if to himself: "Oh, Ma, Ma, what a grace you have given me," raising his hands in prayer. His eyes filled with tears, and he turned to me.

"You see what she does to me? I can't even speak of her without weeping."

He collected himself and went on, his voice different now, older, more hushed.

"In 1974 I took Ma back to Pondicherry to live with me in the ashram. In the next months Ma had great visions, one after the other. Gradually I realized that Ma was the Mother of the coming Great Transformation, the Mother to whom Aurobindo and Sweet Mother had given the task of preparing humankind for its next evolutionary stage, which will be the establishment of divine life on earth. Vision by vision the great task unfolded along with her role in it. Ma accepted everything naturally; she had always known who she is. I told no one, no one at all. I did not want Ma's progress to be interfered with.

"Then I thought it essential for Ma to have some formal education. I took her to Hyderabad and put her into a girls' hostel. This was a mistake. Ma did not want to study. Her mind is far above ours.

"I took Ma back to my village at the end of 1975. She was often in *samadhi*—complete absorption in the Infinite. Sometimes she would be in trance for fourteen hours without a break. I became afraid. I had sole responsibility for her and there she was in trance almost all day, sleeping and eating little. You see her now, so fresh and beautiful. You have no idea what her body has been through; you have no conception of her sacrifice."

His voice was shaking. "What she has endured is beyond words. I *saw* it. I saw the trances, the days of pain. She was always uncomplaining. Always, always without any self-pity. Anyone else would have been finished by a fifteenth part of what she endured."

He clenched both fists as if in anger at what she had had to suffer.

"At that time she was very fragile. I did not want anyone to see her. I knew she needed to be alone with her work. Some villagers did come and worship her. They would just come and sit with her and worship her and go away when she had come out of trance. But no one was informed; no one was told anything. The goddess Durga advised me through Ma not to leave her alone and I didn't.

"In 1978 I took Ma back to Pondicherry. She was healthy, clear, able to be in trance continually without showing it. I began therefore to speak about her. In June of that year a group of ashramites came and interviewed her and were moved. They were not prepared to accept her completely, but then it would have taken a great deal of courage to do so. Then Western and other Indian devotees started coming."

He looked over at me. "Now tell me—do you understand everything? Is everything perfectly clear?"

Sweat was pouring down my face.

"It will take me many years really to understand," I managed.

"Yes," he said. "But a beginning has been made, no? Here I am and here you are. We can go on talking. And you will be here with Ma, and Ma herself will open you."

It was late afternoon. The room was full of shadows. "I am tired," Mr. Reddy said, appearing for the first time crumpled. I had not stopped to think how much I must be exhausting a sick man, and he had not given his sickness another thought.

"Forgive me," I said. "I have made you talk on and on."

"Talking about the Mother keeps me alive," he said, and walked slowly out.

I sat on in the darkening room. Did I really understand what Mr. Reddy was saying? Could I really follow it? Did I, in fact, truly believe it? What would it take to *believe* that Meera was the incarnation of the Divine Mother? What would it take to silence the doubts, cynical asides, and fears that had also surfaced as he was speaking?

The rest of the day passed in turmoil. Just before I slept that night I heard a voice say softly, as if from above my pillow: *You are in a new world. Your old mind will not help you.*

The next day I was sitting in the drawing room of Ma's house, reading, looking up from time to time at a photograph of her on the mantelpiece.

All at once a clear, very bright gold light started to stream from it. I froze in my chair. I blinked several times. The light did not go away. In fact, it grew brighter, so bright I could not see Ma's face in the photograph at all. I looked around at the chair, the sofa, the desk, my hands, and then back to the photo. The Light was still there, still burning.

This went on for twenty minutes.

Mr. Reddy then came in, noticed I was looking pale, and asked kindly: "Are you tired? Don't read so much."

I told him what had happened.

"Gold light is the Light of Illumined Mind," Mr. Reddy said matter-of-factly. "The Divine Mother uses several lights for healing and instruction. You will see them all."

And he sat down and read the paper.

ॐ The house where Mr. Reddy and Ma were staying in Kakinada had a large open roof, like that of the house of my childhood in Delhi. It was delightful to walk on it in the late afternoon. Ma often came. Mr. Reddy and I would stroll arm in arm joking or talking Hindu philosophy; Ma and Adilakshmi would walk around, usually silently, in their own time.

That day Ma was wearing a white sari. Her hair was less strictly combed back than usual, and she looked wild, almost angry. The afternoon darkened. A storm was beginning, one of the rapid noisy thunderstorms that characterizes an Indian monsoon. Lightning crackled on the horizon. No one else seemed to notice, and the walk on the roof continued.

Ma sat down, with her back to the storm. I sat on the edge of the roof next to her. We were looking into each other's eyes. The whole sky had now turned a dark purple-gray. Her eyes were larger than ever, boiling with energy. I felt frightened but could not turn away. Suddenly the entire horizon behind her from one end of the sky to the other broke into a vast flame of lightning and a thunderclap so loud I wanted to cry out.

What I saw, as clearly and precisely as I have seen anything, was that the great unfurling of lightning was in her body. In the second of the explosion of lightning I saw her in outline on the edge of vanishing altogether, but with the whole of the purple sky and the zigzag of lightning inside her.

The storm ceased as quickly as it had begun. No rain came, and the sky cleared with eerie speed. Ma said something quiet to Adilakshmi, got up, and went downstairs.

I stayed up on the roof. In Pondicherry, in the early days, I had seen Ma, while kneeling to her at *darshan*, as vast with all the stars and suns inside her body. But this had been a kind of gentle dream. Now she had shown me—what? Herself. For those seconds I had been allowed to see her Divine Being in its splendor.

My mind went white. I sat on the side of the roof in the same place Ma had sat. Evening was coming in over the houses; a dog was scratching itself in the courtyard below. Somewhere in the distance, a radio was blaring film songs.

Early the next morning I read for the first time these words in Aurobindo: "Love is a passion and it seeks for two things, eternity and intensity, and in the relation of the lover and the Beloved the seeking for eternity and for intensity is instinctive and self-born. . . . Passing beyond desire for possession, which means a difference, it is a seeking for oneness, of two souls merging into each other."

I wrote Aurobindo's words down in the yellow notebook I had with me, realizing I had been given them as a sign and a task. I had recognized something none of the lies or evasions of the years to come could entirely efface; recognized, as if by the light of one of those lightnings that had broken from her body, that She was my soul's Beloved, and that the meaning of my life lay in love for Her.

On the walk to Ma's house next morning I wondered how she would next appear. She was sitting on the veranda, shelling peas with Adilakshmi. Her hair was down, and she was rubbing her eyes a little sleepily.

I sat down by them. After a while Ma went in, and Adilakshmi and I went on shelling the peas. That morning we had our first long conversation. Adilakshmi is a stately, radiant woman, then in her middle thirties. She wore a deep gold sari and gold bangles on both wrists, which made her very beautiful. I told her so.

"Mother is the beautiful one," she said, looking down.

I asked her if she ever wanted to marry.

"No," she answered. "I always wanted to live with the Divine, even as a child. I always knew I would. I used to dream of living on an ashram. As a young girl I used to dream of living with a god."

She smiled at my astonishment.

"We in India do not think the gods are far. They are all around us. They walk our streets; they come to us in dreams. I always had to find God, or die."

We went on shelling peas. "When I was twenty-five, after getting a philosophy degree, I just left home. I took a train, saying to myself that if God existed he would look after me!"

"You mean to tell me that you, a daughter of a good family—"

"Very good family," Adilakshmi corrected me.

"You mean to tell me you just got onto a train to look for God?"

"Yes," Adilakshmi said. "With one hundred rupees and no saris. I have always been mad. If I had not been mad, I would never have left home. If I had never left home, I would not have found her. So madness is a good thing, no?"

I nodded helplessly.

"In the train I saw myself protected by lions and tigers."

I started to laugh.

"And where were you going on this heroic train journey protected by lions and tigers?"

"What did it matter where I was going! The important thing was to leave home. The *most* important thing was to find God. Actually I was going to Pandaripur, a pilgrimage center for Krishna. Suddenly, instead of asking for a ticket to Pandaripur, I said, 'Pondicherry.' I arrived in Pondy, went to the ashram, and the first person I met was Mr. Reddy. He was standing at the ashram gate. He had made a mistake about the time of a class he was giving (he used to teach telugu). I looked at him and thought, This man is the person I am searching for: He will take me to God."

I stared at Adilakshmi.

"Just like that?"

"Just like that. Mr. Reddy took me to his home, where his wife gave me a sari, and then I came back to the samadhi, the tomb of Aurobindo, where I had a very, very beautiful experience." Adilakshmi smiled at the memory.

"I knelt by the tomb and saw clearly a beautiful old man with long white hair and a fractured leg in splints come toward me and embrace me."

"You did not know that Aurobindo at the end of his life had a broken leg?"

"Of course not. I knew nothing about Aurobindo. Sometime later he gave me vision after vision of the inner meaning of 'Savitri,' his poem about the Mother. He would tell me to look up line so-and-so after the vision, and there I would see everything I had seen written."

Adilakshmi spoke with the same unnerving directness and simplicity as did Mr. Reddy.

"Sweet Mother accepted me into the ashram in 1969. I loved her very much. I was very depressed when she left the body in 1973. Then Mr. Reddy told me about Mother Meera." Adilakshmi gazed down at the floor.

"Mr. Reddy is a wonderful man," she said. "He has saved my life many, many times. Through him I met Ma in 1974.

"The first time I saw Meera I loved her. She was fourteen, so thin and elegant and smartly dressed. She had such big open eyes. I had always wanted to give myself to God; I recognized the Divine in her and so decided to offer her everything. At that time Ma was staying with Mr. Reddy in Pondy. Every day we would see each other.

"How beautiful those days were! When I wasn't teaching—I taught English at the ashram—I would be with Mr. Reddy and her. She was only fourteen, and yet she had the calm and presence of mind of an old man. Whatever she did she did perfectly. And she was so kind. I felt her greatness immediately; but it was her humility that made me love her."

Adilakshmi's eyes filled with tears, which she brushed away with her gold sleeve. "To have so much power and be so humble? How is it possible?"

Her tears fell.

"I met Ma again in 1976. When I saw her that time she was wearing a blue dress. Immediately, with open eyes, I saw her as Krishna."

"Krishna?" I said, surprised, remembering the experience in Ladakh.

"All forms are the Mother. The Divine Mother has the whole universe in her." Adilakshmi opened her arms very wide. "All the gods are in her. Where would the male gods be without the Shakti, the female power that creates everything? Many people have seen Ma in different forms. Some as Sri Aurobindo, some as the Virgin Mary. It is normal."

"Normal?" I laughed.

"Yes," said Adilakshmi firmly. "One day all the things that seem so wild and strange to you now will seem normal."

She stood up to go in.

"Isn't it hard, Adilakshmi, to worship Ma? I, too, have seen some small parts of her power, but how to connect that with the young girl we see every day, sewing, shopping, walking in the drive?"

Adilakshmi burst out laughing.

"But that is the mystery, isn't it?"

"How do you worship Ma?"

"As she is. Simply as she is."

She turned and was about to leave when I said: "You realize how the world could view you and Mr. Reddy?"

"Oh, yes," she said, turning back to face me. "They would see us as mad fantasists. Two people with a divine dream projecting it onto a small, innocent girl. Something stupid like that."

"But how do you know that Ma is divine?" I said in my rational "Oxford" voice.

Adilakshmi clapped her hands. "How do I know? By continual living experience. How else? I live with Ma; I see her sometimes twenty-two hours of the day. I know she is absolutely unlike me. The more I know her, the deeper I wonder at her. I am not a stupid love-drunk person. I watch; I observe. Do you imagine I would give up my life to her had I not known? Would I and Mr. Reddy have risked everything, given up respectability, money, position, the ashram, our whole world, had we not been certain?" She paused. "Andrew, I never try to convince anyone of anything. The great mysteries have to be experienced. They have to be lived. The only way to reach anyone really is to offer your life. That is what Ma is doing. She is not talking, justifying. She is giving herself completely, at every second, in every way. Just giving herself. Those with eyes to see will see. Those who dare to know will know. I try to offer my life also."

She paused. "And now I must go in and make lunch."

I thought, after Adilakshmi had left, of the old woman I had seen at Mahabalipuram worshipping the lingam as the sea poured over her. The joy on her face and on Adilakshmi's were the same joy—that of surrender. Adilakshmi and Mr. Reddy had given all they had to Ma. By their love and its mad courage they had both crossed over into a dimension of humble happiness.

Mr. Reddy and Adilakshmi were both whole human beings. Their sacrifice—if that was the right word—had not made them narrow or unaware of the world. Adilakshmi's beauty, exuberance, and wit were not at all characteristic of the shriveled ashramite women I had seen. Nothing seemed extinguished in her. And although Mr. Reddy was sick, his whole being emanated peace.

Seeing their delight so clearly made me sad. Adilakshmi and Mr. Reddy were so Indian—Indian in their spiritual passion, their daring, their exultation in renunciation of the world for God. My Indian childhood made me understand them intuitively; but my Western training and ambition distanced me from their innocence. I realized that my road to Ma would be crooked; it would not have the honest straightness I admired in theirs.

I said this later to Mr. Reddy.

He laughed. "A zigzag path gets there in the end, no? And the best police, you know, are reformed thieves."

He tickled my neck. "Don't always be so serious. *Some* seriousness is good. But remember to play with the Mother also."

He whispered, "I am doing nothing but playing with Ma. Is that a serious thing for a dignified old man to be doing? Oh, and I used to be so very serious."

Ma came in and Mr. Reddy said something to her in Telugu. She answered and then retired.

"What did you say?" I asked.

"I said to Ma, 'You have made a very happy small boy out of a serious and dignified old man.' "

"And what did Ma say?"

"If I was not always a child, I would never have found the Mother."

"So Ma wins?"

"Ma always wins. In the great Divine Game, the one who loves most wins. And who loves more than the Mother?"

Ma reentered and stood by his chair. "Ma," he said, "Ma,

give me the words to tell this young man how loving you are.
Give me words beautiful enough."

That night, back at the hotel, I fell quickly into deep
sleep. All night in dreams, the image of a sculpture I
had loved in a temple in Mahabalipuram—of the goddess
Durga slaying Mahisasura, the Buffalo demon—kept coming
back to me, and with such insistence I knew I was being told
something. When I woke, I remembered what I had read in
the local guidebook; this sculpture is the illustration of the
"Devi Mahatmyam," an epic poem about the Goddess, which
I had made a note of to read. I looked all over Kakinada for
a copy of the work and at last, in the most unlikely and grimy
of bookshops, I found one. It was the last copy, the man said,
that he would ever have in stock. "I am going out of business,"
he said. "No one reads now."

The "Devi Mahatmyam" is a glorification of the Divine
Mother and an account of her creation and conquest of the
supreme asura and demon of destruction, who threatens the
creation.

I sat out in the noisy street and opened it at random.

"By you this universe is borne, by you this world is created.
By you it is protected, O Devi, and you always consume it in
the end."

I saw Ma sitting with the whole horizon blazing behind her.

I opened the book again. The gods are told that Mahisasura
has usurped the functions and powers of many of their number
and is threatening the cosmos:

Having thus heard the words of the devas,
Vishnu was angry and also Shiva, and their
faces became fierce with frowns.

Then issued forth a great light from the face
of Vishnu, who was full of intense anger, and
from that of Brahma and Shiva, too. From the
bodies of Indra and other devas also sprang
forth a very great light. And all this light
united together.

The devas saw there a *concentration of light like
a mountain blazing excessively,* pervading all the
quarters with its flames. Then that unique
light, produced from the bodies of all the devas, pervading the three worlds with its luster,
combined into one and became a female form.

Sitting in the dirt, with bicycles ringing around me and car
horns blaring, I felt my body fill with bliss. Then with extreme
urgency messages came.

*Mahisasura is the madness of the human mind without God—
the mind that is destroying the planet; the mind that made and
used the atomic bomb; the mind that is everywhere creating a
wrecked, starved world in its own psychic image.*

*The gods have created me, the Mother, out of all their different
lights so this evil can be destroyed. Destroyed not with cruelty but
with the power of love and gnosis.*

I tried to get up three times, but my legs buckled under
me. I found myself, my head in my hands, saying over and
over the different names of the Divine Mother that I knew,
Brahmani, Mahesvari, Virgin Mary, Fatima, Neit, Isis, Saraswati, Kali, Meera.

*I am above all names and all worlds and all forms. Open the
book again.* I opened to: "Whenever trouble arises . . . I shall
incarnate and destroy all enemies."

Again I saw Ma: face and body on the roof, the sky on fire
behind her. This time she was smiling with the same triumphant
passion as she had in the doorway in Pondicherry.

ॐ Next day I woke up determined to ask Ma for an interview. I had to talk to her. I had only two days left before I went back to Oxford. I asked Mr. Reddy to ask Ma for me.

He went into the room where Ma was and returned. "Ma will talk to you this afternoon."

I felt sick to the stomach at myself, at all the doubts and fears I knew still accompanied my love for her. I felt weak so sat down in a chair and put my face in my hands.

Mr. Reddy sat down on the sofa beside me and took my hand.

"All this is very bewildering to the mind," I said. "I've been given so much. Why can't I give myself completely?"

I stared at the dark green marble floor, awash in sunlight.

"To give yourself completely to the Mother is complete realization," Mr. Reddy whispered. "It can take many lives."

"Everything has to be changed, doesn't it?—every habit, every way of thinking."

"Yes." He smiled. "It is a long work. But it is the only real work. And Ma is here to help you. She is *here*. She is in the other room as we speak, cooking lunch. Follow her and she will be your Master, your Mother, your Beloved, your Friend. She will become everything to you as she has become everything to me. And when she is everything to you, you will know her in everything."

He started to cough and looked suddenly frail. He saw me looking at him with concern and looked back mischievously.

"This illness, too, is only Ma's play, her maya."

Either this man is mad, I thought, or he is illumined. There is no other possible explanation.

"I am not illumined completely," Mr. Reddy said out loud, reading my thought. "But Ma has lit some lamps in my brain that nothing can put out."

. . .

The hours before seeing her I spent in prayer. I remembered something Thuksey Rinpoche had once said: "The great enemy to spiritual progress is the belief you know already. Knowledge is unfolded. Pray to be willing, at every stage to be ignorant, so you can be really taught."

How would I learn *that* ignorance rather than rely on the learned ignorance of years of habit, assumption, intellectual formulation?

Mr. Reddy, Adilakshmi, and I waited for Ma in the drawing room. A late red-gold light filled the room.

She came in silently in a white sari, not smiling, and sat in the chair opposite me, gazing down. I had thought I was calm, until she entered, but her beauty and her majesty made me tremble.

"Ma," I began.

"Andrew," she said, looking up.

As she said my name for the first time a sob arose in me and shook my entire body. I tried to control it, but my whole being started to weep before her. The grief of my life's loneliness, guilt, and sexual pain seemed to seize me and pour itself out at her feet.

I wept for a long time. Slowly, in the huge and healing silence of her presence, I began to feel calm.

"I came before you with questions. But now I understand I only wanted to weep before you and sit with you."

Mr. Reddy translated.

Ma smiled.

Another long silence began, golden this time with the light that was filling the room, covering the chairs, Ma's hands, the floor between me and her. I knew I should not speak, just open and wait.

Ma gazed at the pearl ring on her right hand.

A calm bliss filled my body.

The tears began again. This time they were tears of relief and joy, with no grief in them at all.

I began to speak haltingly.

"You have always been guiding me, haven't you?"

"Yes."

"You were in Pondicherry living quietly with Mr. Reddy when I first came there. It was you who, with Aurobindo, opened my mind; it was you who prepared me to meet you."

"Yes."

"In these last weeks I feel you have been revealing to me your divine Self. Is this true?"

"Yes."

"Can I receive your Light?"

"You are receiving it. One day you will see it."

I trembled. "You have come to save the world, haven't you?"

"Yes. There are others working here, too."

"What can I do to help your work?"

"Realize yourself."

There was nothing else to say. I sat gazing at Ma with astonishment, and she gazed calmly back. After one last long silence she smiled and rose.

I went over and knelt at her feet.

Two days later Mr. Reddy accompanied me to the station.

As we parted, he said: "Ramakrishna said, 'The Master is like a cobra. If he bites you, you die.' Ma has bitten you. You will die."

"I want to die," I said fervently.

"Do you really?" Mr. Reddy asked quietly. "We shall see."

# FOUR

After all I had been given by Ma, after all I had experienced, I ran from her. I saw her only twice, briefly, in the seven years between 1980 and 1987. In 1983 I moved to Paris and did not write to Ma or phone her when she came to live only an hour's plane journey away in Germany; I did not communicate with her when Mr. Reddy died in 1985 after a long bout with kidney disease, which I had done nothing to try to help alleviate; I never sent her the books I was writing, which my experience with her had in many ways inspired; I did not change my life in any significant way to practice what she had begun to teach me.

I gave myself every possible excuse for this behavior. I was still young, too young to do the hard solitary work her Yoga demanded. I was an "artist" and needed to develop my "art" and engineer my "career." All the energy and clarity I might have devoted to her I devoted to my books, my teaching, a series of wasteful and hysterical affairs with men and women in which I tried to find again the love I had glimpsed in her.

The most successful evasion of Ma was to pretend during all this time that I did still love her. I kept her photograph with me always; I talked about her; I wrote a book about Ladakh, several novels that explored the nature and cost of spiritual life. The truth was that I was more anxious to talk about spiritual love than to live it, more able to exploit the split in my personality between the worldly and the spiritual than to do the work of healing it, hungry for recognition as "a spiritual person" without being brave enough to realize that recognition is meaningless.

The years after Kakinada were what the world calls successful but full of private torment and bewilderment. I lost myself in a series of roles I played too well to be able to abandon—of teacher, coffee-table mystic, writer, nomad, lover. My life was never more repetitive and empty than when I pretended I was the master of it, filling it with diversion, travel, creation; I stayed fixed in the paralysis of a long evasion of the one authentic passion of my life, while deploying all the gorgeous vocabulary of spiritual transformation. At the center of everything I did was a great lie, a lie of fear, my fear of her, and my fear of my love for her. Everything was subtly falsified by that fear—my emotional life, and my art—and the falsifications became more garish and elaborate as I became more evasive. No one told me; no one could: I had covered the traces of the path to her so well, few people even knew it existed. My lie was so pervasive that I almost ceased to think about it; it had become the air I breathed.

Ma let me run through my games until I had none left that I could believe in; she let me enact my fantasies of success and passion until I could see exactly how hollow and self-annihilating they each were.

My flight from Ma ended with the disastrous end of a nine-month-long extremely destructive love affair with L, a Californian whom I had met in New York and taken to Ladakh and South India. L and I knew how to torture and shame each other, how exactly to play on each other's weaknesses. I hated

L's promiscuous and exploitative past; he hated my judgment of him. I was ashamed of my addiction to him since I did not respect him; I knew I was being used but was held to the relationship by a desire to achieve at last some kind of sexual stability, however sordid. When L's and my mutual disgust descended into physical violence in Spain in the winter of 1986, we both realized we had to part, or risk killing each other. I returned alone to Paris in early January 1987 and fell ill with pneumonia.

During a week of fear and despairing illness the realization came to me that I could not continue as my old self.

I had exhausted my capacity to believe in anything, in love or "success" or "art." My relationship with L had terrified me by its perversity: My rage at what L had done to me—at what I had allowed him to do—had become murderous and all-consuming; this shocked me into seeing finally how little my success as an artist had healed the self-hatred my early abandonment by my mother had bred in me. I could not continue my life as I had lived it away from Ma; I had to take the journey with her, and take it with total commitment, or go on repeating the same evasions and desperations, endlessly and purposelessly.

I rang Ma. "I cannot live without you," I told her.

"No," she replied in the clear English she had learned since I last saw her.

"Can I come and stay in your house?"

"You can stay as long as you like," she said.

After the bitterness and horror of the previous years the warmth of her low voice brought tears to my eyes, and for a while I could not speak.

"Will you heal me and show me my true self?"

"Yes."

"I have been away from you a long time."

"You have always been with me."

A long pause, then her voice came, very young and gentle. "Are you coming this Friday?"

"I am coming." I asked her again: "Heal me."

"Yes," she said.

I put down the phone. A wave of power, of solid wild power, made me lie down on the floor. I had been in bed for a week with pneumonia, hardly able to move. The next morning—Wednesday—I felt cured and strong. I went and bought my tickets for Frankfurt.

In the plane I remembered Thuksey Rinpoche that final summer I had been with him in Ladakh in 1981 when he was dying. A German woman—one of his students—had said:

"Is enlightenment painful?"

"Enlightenment is not painful. How could it be?"

"Is the process toward enlightenment painful?"

"Yes."

"Is this pain necessary?"

"Yes. One life has to end for another to begin. The ego has to die for awareness to be born. The ego does not die fast."

Then he said, "The misery you will have to endure in realizing enlightenment is nothing to the misery you will endure in life after life if you do not realize it. To get an arrow out of the flesh, you have to probe the wound. That hurts. But be grateful that you have understood enough to choose this misery. Not just grateful, be happy. It is important to be happy."

Solemnly he looked at each of us and said: "However many times you fall, stand up. However many times you come close to despair, go on trusting. However many times your heart wants to close, keep it open."

Two days later Ma and I were sitting in her small, square drawing room at the top of her four-story house in Thalheim. She had been out for a walk in the cold but cloudless afternoon. Mud from the melting snow had splashed the bottom of her red slacks.

She caught my eyes looking at the mud and smiled.

I felt such deep joy at being with her I could say nothing for a long time.

"Forgive me," I said at last.

She gazed into my eyes.

"Nothing to forgive," she said.

"The best in me loves you more than life itself."

"I know," she said.

"Help me at last to understand you."

"You will understand," she said softly.

Clear winter sunlight filled the room.

"Without you my life would have been extremely dark."

She laughed. "But I was in your life. Your life brought you here."

"I am here because of your grace. I know that. If I have the courage to stay, it will be by your grace. If I have the strength to continue your work, that also will be by your grace."

She looked at her hands.

"That is true?" I pressed her.

"It is true. But you have your strength also."

"I have no patience, no clarity, no love."

"If you did not have patience, how could you write? If you did not have clarity, you would not be here. If you had no love, you would not be with me."

I looked at the great red bear on the sideboard beside her with its puffy heart and the words "I love you" written on it.

"I want to ask you about Grace," I began again.

She looked at me with her great, wide, quiet eyes, and a peace fell between us.

"Your grace burned away my illusions. You gave me what I thought I wanted to show me it meant nothing."

"Yes."

"You have ended my life in the world."

"Yes."

"This was a great grace."

"Yes."

There was a long, calm silence.

"Being away from you," I said, "was like being in an old Indian plane going very much too fast. Everything shook."

She laughed. "And the lights went out?"

"And the lights went out . . . I thought the plane was going to crash."

"But it brought you here, no?"

"And that was where it was going all along."

She nodded and looked out the window.

"Some planes are difficult to land," she said. "They hit the runway and shake from side to side." She shook her hands in the air.

"You took me," I said, "on a wild journey."

"You are wild." A pause. "But you are here, no?"

It was the second time she had said it. I was here. What was the point of going over the past, of regretting anything? For a brief moment I saw a great burning white light around her. It was as bright as it had been in Pondicherry, in the doorway. And as I saw it I heard the voice inside me: *This is the beginning; this is only the beginning.*

Then she said out loud: "This is only the beginning."

I was startled.

She smiled. I was to see that tender, amused smile often in the next months.

Mother got up, went into the kitchen next door to get some water for the plants on the windowsill.

"I feel at home at last."

"You are home," she said.


I went downstairs to my room on the floor below and sat a long time with my head in my hands. I thought of the words of the Katha Upanishad: "There is the path of joy and there is the path of pleasure. Pondering on them, the wise [one] chooses the path of joy; the fool takes the path of pleasure." In my youth I had the strength and grief to choose the path of joy; then worldliness, fear, and ambition diverted me from it. But she had, despite myself, kept me true to my deep self, brought me by winding alleys to the open river I thought I had lost forever. I remembered eight years before, panicking in an afternoon crowd in Mathura, in the noise and fury of an Indian summer afternoon. I bolted down a long, dark street. At the end of it, I found myself staring at the Ganges clear and quiet in the reddening sun. A boatman emerged from the shadows of a ruined temple and I, as if in a dream, traveled down the river until evening fell.

I was on the river again, and Ma was the boatman. The light in my room in Germany and the light that afternoon in India were the same light, lucid and golden.

And now, as on that afternoon years ago, I had to surrender, to yield to the rhythm of the water, to lie down and let myself be carried downriver.

After the panic, the rage, the baffled distress—this great, wide, extravagant light.

Then began the most extreme of any of the experiences she had yet given me.

I was shown a film of my life. Everything was in it, with the scalding vividness of a dream, a dream lit by the same gold light as was flooding the afternoon. I lived through my childhood in India, the pain of my relationship with my mother, with England, the horror of school, my adulthood in Oxford, the meeting with the Rinpoche—in short powerful bursts, in waves of such energy and such anguish I almost fainted. I was not merely watching the film; I was in the film. I was the film. And I was able for the first time to understand why everything had happened as it had. I saw why I had been born in India but reared in England, why my life had been split so completely between East and West, male and female, heart and intellect; I saw exactly how she had made the film, turned it, filled it— how everything had proceeded with a fierce precision, a breath-taking and marvelous skill. Watching, I felt again and again the cutting, the slashing of her surgeon's knife, of her sculptor's hammer—why she had cut that, shattered that, shaped with repeated wild, accurate hammer blows this and that. I wondered at her work; I wondered how I had survived it; I wondered at the energy and strength with which she had repeatedly graced me to be able to survive such violent, fast work. I laughed out loud, wept as I have never wept before or since, with ecstasy at what she had done, at its divine ruthlessness, its terrible mercy. And I realized as I laughed and wept that the film was now over. I had been allowed to see it. I had been allowed to die in this life. I had been allowed for those brief, amazing seconds a total glimpse into the shape of my ego, of my biography, of the necessities that had impelled its suffering. And in all the grief, in all the horror, I had been allowed to see only her grace, her love, her power.

It was the most terrifying experience of my life. I fell on the floor, howled out loud as if I were being cut to pieces.

I heard the words *You are nothing; you are no one; you are my child; you are me*, first separately, then together—paradox circling paradox.

Then, almost insolently, everything returned to normal. I sat like a child on my bed dangling my feet, studying the red-and-gold pattern of the bedspread, listening to the traffic of the evening outside.

ॐ That night I dreamed of an American friend who teaches with me at Hobart. We were walking by a lake and he was dancing, slowly, hilariously, singing out of key a Bach sarabande we both loved. I woke up laughing and wondered why I had dreamed of him. Then I remembered a story he had told me the spring before, one gloomy Sunday toward the end of term.

"When I was a young man I worked in New York for a while. I wanted the high life; I wanted to succeed. But I realized the city was mad and I was becoming mad in it. I fled to the place I imagined would be the most different from everything I had known—Hawaii.

"Imagine me, a depressive, overeducated atheistic Jew in Hawaii! It was wonderful; I lived with a native family unlike any people I had ever known or even believed could exist. They were half-naked most of the time, naturally spiritual, as I imagine the natives of India were in your childhood. I loved them and they loved me.

"After I had been with them a few months, the head of the family told me he would like to introduce me to the family whale. He said there was a whale the family revered that would come when called to play with anyone in the clan, at a secret place on the island. " 'It is very simple. You wait in the water. The whale senses your presence, appears, and comes toward you.' " They called the whale the Mother of the family.

"I thought the man was nuts and that the time had come to leave the genial madhouse in Hawaii before this brain I had trained so assiduously for years finally dissolved.

"But I loved the man and did not want to hurt him, so I agreed to go to the secret place. The next afternoon the whole family accompanied us to a group of rocks in a bay. Everyone was drunk and joking; I felt happy just to be with them and felt that even if I was being fooled, I did not mind. I liked these people; they could have their fun with a white man if they wanted—it was all right by me. Then I remembered that I can't swim. I told the man.

" 'Don't worry,' " he said. " 'Just cling to the rock I'll show you. The whale will do the rest.'

"We arrived at the rocks; I stripped and lowered my pale, and by now trembling, body into the water. His family started singing behind me.

"Then, the most astonishing single thing of my life happened, the thing I would have disbelieved if anyone else had told me it was possible. About five hundred yards away the biggest black whale I have ever seen calmly arose from the waters. Its glistening ebony back lay in the sun. That single moment overturned everything I had ever thought of as reality. I was terrified. I could not swim and I was immersed, clinging to this tiny rock. But then I felt it, I felt the whale feeling my terror and sending toward me these great warm, healing waves of energy, pure energy. How can I explain this? What words are there? I knew, with certainty, that the whale had felt my terror, knew I could not swim, and was sending me through the sunlit water, wave after wave of what I can only call love, a silent, strong, immense, impersonal love. I had only to receive this energy and everything would be all right.

"The whale started to move. It was some time before I understood what she was doing. She was moving horizontally, very slowly and calmly, coming a few feet closer each time, so I wouldn't be swamped and drowned.

"She came to within two feet of me. I was so overwhelmed I had no idea what to do next. The head of the family came onto the rock behind me and started stroking the back of my head. " 'Go on,' " he said, chuckling, " 'touch the Mother. Touch her. Don't you want to touch your Mother?' " I put my hand out and touched her.

"The whale rolled over onto her belly and let me run my hand along it, as if I were her own child, nuzzling against her.

Then, calmly, she withdrew. I felt as she moved so silently away that she was only moving away in time, in 'biography.' In the dimension where we had at last met, and which she had opened to me, there was no time, no parting, no coming and going. There we would always be together."

ॐ For me, also, the unimaginable had happened; the whale of bliss, of the Mother in her splendor, had surfaced. I, too, was in the warm water, frightened at times, unable to swim, but clinging to the rock. I, too, felt the rich waves of Love coming through the water to me from Her—in a hundred secret movements daily, in sudden moments of bliss, in meditations where my mind fell away, in a new wild, fresh sensing of everything, in the love that danced between me and her whenever we met. And my friend's story showed me what I must do—stay in the water and not move. Accept with every movement and every breath, the wild, sweet power she was pouring into me.

On the fifth day, I met Ma in the kitchen in her blue gardening coat and started to say something. My voice failed me, and the tears fell. She gazed at me calmly, saying nothing, her soft eyes wide with compassion, staying near me just long enough to flood me with such bliss I had to sit down, take my head in my hands, and start to laugh.

I went back into my room, opened the book of Bengali mystical poetry by Ramprasad that I had brought with me, and read:

In heaven there is a fair of madmen
Who will ever fathom
The mystery of the Play of Love . . .
You are mad with love, O Mother, Crown of madmen . . .

🕉 The next day I met her on the stairs in the afternoon, carrying shopping bags from Massa, the supermarket. She smiled mischievously.

I said, "Do I have your permission to go absolutely mad?"

She laughed. "Yes. Mr. Reddy was mad, no? If he had not been mad, he would not have found me in his own house."

"And now I am in your house going mad in you."

"It is nice, no?"

Her voice was small, childlike.

All morning I had been unable to leave my room because of the wild happiness that possessed me. Even the small pink plastic animals dangling from the wall above my bed had seemed miracles of beauty, as if made by Cellini.

"Yes, it is nice."

She walked upstairs slowly, turning once to look back amusedly.

I went back into my room and stood a long time at the window. A light delicate snow was falling over the whole world, purifying everything.

🕉 *Thalheim* means, appropriately, "valley home." It is a small, unremarkable German village in Hesse, about an hour's drive from Frankfurt, set in a valley and surrounded by low green hills and forests. It has a church with a large, obvious spire, one post office, one bank, two winding main streets, a few shops, a stream often turgid with rainwater. The predominant house colors are gray and gray-beige; the gardens are tidy—frequently studded with plastic gnomes. Everyone seems to be in bed by nine o'clock. The most beautiful thing in Thalheim is the cemetery—a large spacious one on a hill, where Mr. Reddy now lies, in the only white marble grave in a sea of black slabs. At night the only signs of life are the white candles burning by the graves in their red plastic containers. There is no cinema, no restaurant, no hotel. In one pub up the road the local boys stroke their mustaches and talk in loud voices; in HUNTING REST PLACE, near Mother's house, tepid coffee is served against a large, blown-up photograph of autumn woods. An almost surreal silence reigns in the village during the day, as if everyone in it were recovering from a long illness.

For all its banality Thalheim is a perfect setting for Ma. Her house is large and comfortable, with a barn that a disciple turned into a workshop, one garden at the back, and another for vegetables in the front. Mother can live the life she likes— quiet and ordinary, going out only to shop or visit the doctor. The village has accepted her. Once only during carnival time a group of local boys paraded up and down outside the house shouting *"Mutter Meera, wo bist du?"* (Mother Meera, where are you?), but only for a few minutes and without any true aggression. Ma is free to do what she wants—to get up when she wants, to garden when she wants (if the grisly German weather permits), to go for long slow walks in the woods. *Darshan* is on Friday, Saturday, Sunday, and Monday evenings. Everything is orderly, unfussy, low-key.

And behind this facade the great Work goes on. It is a beautiful joke, and I grew to appreciate it. Very early on I took as my motto for life in Thalheim the lines from the Tao: "Do that which consists in taking no action; pursue that which is not meddlesome; savor that which has no flavor."

In the many astonishing experiences that followed my return to her, I would walk through Thalheim and think, Well I cannot be making this up, can I? If I were, the awakening to reality—the gardens, the plastic gnomes, the uniform (mostly gray-blue) cars—would soon shake me lucid. "If a visionary experience can survive Thalheim," I wrote to a friend in Paris, "it can survive anywhere."

I came to be very grateful for this ordinariness and to see

Ma's wisdom in surrounding herself with it. I came also to learn from it.

Thalheim compelled me to give up old snobberies, distractions, hungers for beauty, for inspiration: I had nowhere to go but inward. The rain on the streets washed away old memories that would have hindered me; the dullness of the days built up slowly a sensitivity to things I would not have noticed, a gratitude for the smallest details of life—the first flowers in a cement playground, the different shades of rain-gray on asphalt, the color of a woman's head kerchief at the grocers, the odd, gritty singsong of the Hesse accent. Biography lost its hold on my mind; as the days went slowly past I came to forget I had been anywhere else or that I ever had another life at all.

After six days in Ma's home I wrote: "Ma has taken away my mind. She has made it impossible for me to read or think. None of the old solutions to boredom can now work.

"I sleep eight or nine perfect hours, wake and putter about my day, sometimes hardly moving from my bed, sometimes going for slow walks. Lowell wrote, 'Sometimes I feel weak enough to enter heaven.' This weakness *is* heavenly. The events in my day are fresh winter light falling on my blankets, or a fly resting on my hand, or sitting by the window and watching the wind move in the trees behind the small vegetable garden outside. I feel no need to be or do anything anymore. When fear comes that I will never be able to 'do' anything again, I laugh at it, for I know it is trying to prevent this great birth that is taking place within me—this birth of Her-in-me.

"Her house has only one rule—no smoking. Otherwise people are free to do what they want, come and go when they want. For the first time in my life I am *free*. Ma leaves me alone.

She smiles when we meet in the garden or in the kitchen, but she makes no intrusive inquiries as to how I am. Her tact with me has been perfect. Her silence sweeps away everything but the calmest, most elemental meeting. She *knows* who I am and treats me as if I were already illumined, with respect and dignity. She has nothing to prove, and she frees me to have to 'prove' nothing.

"In the questions-and-answers section of the book Adilakshmi is writing about Ma, Ma is asked: 'What should I ask for?'

"Ma replies: 'Ask for everything. Everything. Do not stop at peace of mind or purity of heart or surrender. Demand everything. Don't be satisfied with anything less than everything. Our Yoga is the transformation of human life into Divine Life here on earth; it is a hard Yoga, and it demands those who have the courage to demand everything, to bear everything, and to ask for everything.'

"All my human relationships have buckled under the crazy need I have always had for the complete Experience. Now, at last, she has brought me to her and shown me that in the endless extravagance of the Divine there is no need ever to stop demanding, to stop hungering. For to those who ask shall be given; for those who dare to be hungry the Food will be brought. It is in loving Her that I will finally know the abandon I have looked for in darker places; in burning with love for Her I will be burned with the Fire I have been calling for constantly all my life."

From the beginning I liked Daniel, the other disciple living in the house. There was a ferocity and toughness in this stocky, sad-eyed Yugoslav that attracted me. Daniel is unsentimental, sometimes aggressively so, and delights in the opposing sides of his character—the spiritual epicure and the sandy-haired "bloke" in dungarees who goes out in his dirty red car every day to clean drainpipes. We studied, riled, supported, mocked, enthused each other from the first. He kept me earthed; I helped him stay airborne.

We did not know it then, in those first weeks of our friendship, but Ma was going to send us together on two different but related journeys. The year was going to be as turbulent and revelatory for him as for me.

After my first week in Ma's house I told Daniel I felt totally happy.

"Then *stay*. Let this joy grow. Don't think you're Tarzan of the Spirit and can take on the whole world. You can't. You're recovering from years of craziness. Go slowly. Ma's not in the business of cheap miracles; transformation takes time.

"Another word of advice; I love giving advice. Now that I've given up sex and cigarettes it's my last pleasure. You'll have great experiences if you want them. But Ma works thoroughly. You'll have the experience and then you'll fall down so you have to climb back up to it and make it certain. For a long time you live in a kind of schizophrenic double-consciousness that isn't always pleasant. It isn't easy, this work. And it gets harder. But there's a hell of a lot of joy to make it worth it. Am I scaring you?"

"No."

"Don't disappoint me. I like to flash my yogic muscles."

I remembered something Ramakrishna had said about the necessity of making spiritual experience firm before risking oneself in the world: "So long as the tadpole's tail does not drop off, it can live only in water; when the tail drops off, it can live both in water and on land."

Daniel walked over to the window and pointed at the swollen gray German sky outside.

"There's enough rain around here to suit every frog."

ॐ Although I hardly saw Mother, I saw Adilakshmi often. Every lunchtime she would bring me Indian food on a tray and we would talk.

"So," Adilakshmi said, "how many days have you been back?"

"Eight. It seems like eight minutes or eight years. Time has no meaning here."

"No meaning?" She laughed. "But you have gray hairs now. I can see at least three. I remember you when you were almost a baby."

She put down the tray and looked at me.

"So you came back in the end. Mr. Reddy used to say, 'He will come back. He'll run away and run around and get tired and come back.' "

Suddenly her eyes filled with tears. "I miss Mr. Reddy so much," she said.

"I have been to the white grave Mother has made for him in the cemetery every day. I'm still not sure why. I think to apologize."

"Apologize?"

"He gave me so much. He lavished his wisdom on me. But I was too young and too scared to understand. It will take me many years to understand him."

"It will take," Adilakshmi said, "an experience as deep as his."

We were silent. The voices of children playing rose from the street.

ॐ That evening in *darshan* I prayed to Ma as she held my head between her hands: All my ideas of love are false and limited. Teach me your love. I can only be healed if I become love. Then in a silence her hands gave, the words arose in my mind: *But you are love. I am love and you are me.*

That was the first *darshan* in which I saw the Divine Light around her steadily, burning clear and brilliant white for a full two hours.

Daniel came up to me afterward and put his arm around my shoulder.

"People come here thinking they are going to become great yogis. But Mother makes us what we really want to be."

"And what is that?"

"Children," he said. "I never wanted to grow up. Why be thirty-six when you can be six? A much more inspired age."

He looked into my eyes: "What do you really want?"

"Absolute devotion."

"Don't force it. Let it grow naturally. Love is shy of any kind of force. Oh, my god, I'm preaching again! I don't know where I get the courage, when I'm such a fool."

"You're not a fool," I said.

"Look here, poet—until you're enlightened, you're a fool. Understand?"

"Daniel," I said hesitantly.

"What now?"

"I saw the Light burning around her for about two hours."

"Oh," he said, grinning, "it's when you start shooting out of the body and the whole room sinks in light that things get really interesting."

That night I had a dream whose meaning would unravel over the next months: A child ran out of a strangely illuminated eighteenth-century house onto a lawn and released two small birds into the air. These birds suddenly became larger—one a peacock, the other a dark bird like a raven with a vast black beak. The raven attacked the peacock and a fierce and noisy fight ensued. The two birds dived screaming down into a lake and continued battling. The lake became covered with blood, and I felt extreme fear that the peacock would be killed because I could not see it. Then I saw something struggling to come out of the water on the other side of the lake. It was not a bird; it was a man, naked, exhausted, but marvelously marked with all the colors of the peacock—his skin a luminous turquoise, red and gold circles all around his body. He could hardly stand, but he was alive. He had my face.

Adilakshmi came in next morning to see me. I told her my dream. "The peacock is Saraswati's bird," she said, "the bird of the goddess of poetry and music. The dream shows you that victory will come."

"Victory?"

"The peacock, as well as being the bird of Saraswati, is also the bird of spiritual victory."

"The man was very exhausted in my dream, Adilakshmi."

She smiled: "It is a long fight."

Ma wasn't yet up, so we had time to talk again about Mr. Reddy.

"I wish so much I could speak to Mr. Reddy now, now that I know much more."

"You can learn so, so much from him always," Adilakshmi said. "He loved Ma in every way God can be loved—as a friend, as a Beloved, as a Mother or Father, as a Child. You must try and love her in all those ways. When you are lonely, turn to him for help. You will find he gives it. He helps me all the time. He is always with me."

Then she spoke quietly of the long pain of Mr. Reddy's last illness and of his death.

"In those last years he withdrew more and more completely into Ma. He spent most of his time in meditation, saying her name, even when Ma was in the room. His kidney disease slowly transformed him into a cripple, unable to move without help, but his joy in Ma remained strong always. His only anxiety was for her—that she should be eating properly, that she should be well, that she should have a roof over her head. He had given Ma everything; in those last years Ma gave everything to him. She fed him with her own hands, bathed him, sat with him for hours and hours in the hospital, kept him alive with her Force for five years after the doctors had given up hope. Sometimes he would say he was not really suffering at all; he was in a kind of dream. He had many, many visions during his illness. Once he saw Ma in an enormous auditorium with thousands of people. She was alone on the stage giving *darshan* to everyone. This dream made him happy because he knew his great desire to make her known to the whole world would be fulfilled. Not long before he died, he dreamed of leading a divine army against hostile forces and triumphing against great odds. He realized his illness had made him into a spiritual warrior capable of taking on the worst forces and winning.

"On the day before he entered the hospital for the last time—the eleventh of June, 1985—he sat and listened to all his favorite devotional songs of India. He was very joyful and said how much he loved India and the Indians for keeping alive such love for God. Watching him listen to the music, I realized there was now no difference, no separation between him and the music; pain and love had transformed his whole being into a song to God."

Adilakshmi sat silently a long time, gazing at her hands.

"Mr. Reddy's death affected Ma deeply. For several days afterward she was almost mad with sorrow. She wept passionately at his funeral. With Mr. Reddy gone there was no one left who could really understand and console her. Ma used to say often in those days that she understood why people in India renounce the world when someone close to them dies."

"I see a gravity in Ma's face these days that was not there before."

"It is there. Ma has suffered. Suffering has brought her closer to us. Mr. Reddy's death broke her heart and brought her closer to *our* reality."

She paused. "So much has happened since you were last with us."

She left, and I wept alone for a long time for everything Mr. Reddy had endured as her herald, all the ridicule and humiliation, and at the mysterious beauty of his dying, absorbed in her. And I wept for Ma, too. For the first time in our relationship, I began to think about her suffering. I realized how callous I had been in placing Ma beyond "human" pain and how that had suited an egoistic distance I wanted to keep between us. I did not mind revering Ma, but I was scared of being moved by her, for that would unlock a deeper, more binding and mysterious love, personal as well as transcendental, intimate as well as ecstatic. And from that love, complete in a human as well as spiritual way, I would have no escape.

Hold me fast, I prayed to her; do not let me escape. Take my heart and break it open.

The woods around Thalheim have small wooden watchtowers in them. You climb up a rickety staircase and sit in a small room overlooking trees and sometimes see, when you are lucky, a few deer browsing in the long frosted grass. That afternoon I sat for hours thinking of nothing, watching the late light deepen in the trees. There was a deep peace throughout my body, a peace almost solid in its strength. At times it seemed there was *only* that peace and my body, the trees, the shifting light, the deer that once suddenly ran across the scrub in front of the tower were all projections of its great wide dream.

The next morning Ma and Adilakshmi came into my room a little after ten o'clock. Ma wore a baggy red jersey and a sari Adilakshmi had painted with red roses.

Ma had not visited me before, and I was overcome with joy.

She sat down at the table, shyly, swinging her feet a little. She had thick gold slippers on, the color of the energy I felt circling my body. She looked a little sleepy, and very young, nine or ten years old.

"I am able to do nothing," I said. "You have taken my mind away."

"Yes," Ma said, smiling happily. "It is nice, no?"

A motorbike revved uselessly outside.

"I've been like that motorbike for years, making a lot of noise but going nowhere."

Ma laughed. "But now you are going fast, no?"

"Don't let me stop, Ma. Keep me clear."

"Don't you feel clear?" Her voice was lightly ironic.

I heard within me the words: *Every moment you will be given the clarity to know what is happening.*

"A part of me is in bliss. A part is afraid."

"That is normal."

"Fear belongs to the ego. The ego is made of fear."

"The soul has no fear."

"The soul is a child, your child."

"Yes." Ma smiled wonderfully; her whole face lit up.

"Make my mind a child also."

"In its reality it is already."

The clouds outside parted, and the room filled with quiet sunlight.

"Ma," I said, "I feel I can ask you anything."

"You are in my house, no?"

"In your house in these last days I have been thinking over

everything I have lived with you, everything Mr. Reddy told me."

Ma nodded.

"Once he said your coming to earth meant that humanity was now in a position to collaborate with God in remaking the world, that humankind was at last evolved enough."

"This is true. But humans must be evolved enough to be humble."

"Isn't the Mother shaking her children awake to what they are?"

"Yes."

"She is making human beings aware through great and terrible things, good and evil events, that they cannot solve their problems alone, that they must turn to a higher Mind, a Force that is Love."

"Yes. Love *and* Knowledge."

"And now a race is going on between the evil and the good in humanity, a frightening race . . ."

"Do not be frightened. Be calm. Turn to God."

"Last night I went out into the woods to be alone with you. I sat on a bench overlooking Thalheim. I heard you say within me: 'The Mother is taking the world back into her hands.'"

"This is true."

"Because the Mother can best guide humankind to what it most needs now—love for all things and beings, knowledge of its identity with the Divine?"

"Yes."

"The Mother has willed the Transformation of the earth?"

"Yes."

"That is why you are here."

"Yes. Other Mothers are here also. And Fathers. The Divine is One. All aspects are here to help humankind forward, to give it strength."

"Help me, Ma, to take the journey into this new dimension you are preparing for everyone."

"You will take it," she said calmly.

"Humanity is on a great adventure toward God."

Ma smiled.

"And you are on a great adventure toward humanity."

Adilakshmi said quietly, "Ma is the supreme adventurer. You will find that out."

"When I see you looking so joyful and so beautiful," I said to Ma, "my heart is full and I want to sing."

She stood up, smoothing down the roses on her sari.

"Sing, then!" she said.


When she had left, I placed my face on the chair where she had sat. Daniel came in and saw me kneeling.

"Oh, my god," he said. "Soon you'll be speaking in tongues."


I spent the next days walking in the snowy hills and woods above the village, walking for hours, sitting in the watchtowers watching in the silence the deer come timidly out. I felt my body lighter, more transparent; every sound I heard in the woods I heard with new, sharp, ecstatic ears; the most ordinary sights—a stream running in sunlight, three heaps of earth surrounded by winter flowers, a slim young tree suddenly illuminated with dusk light—became sources of a deep happiness, revelations of her presence, messages of love from her soul to mine. I began to walk in a different way—more slowly, from a higher balance in the body; my most intimate physical rhythms were being subtly changed. Twice, briefly but unmistakably, I saw rose light shimmering on the snow in the fields—a great sudden wash of rose light from nowhere, a dance of

Her bliss, pristine and astounding on the great white lake before me.

It was on the second day of my walks that I began to feel a pressure in the middle of my forehead. At first I thought the silence was exhausting me and my mind wished again to take possession of my self. But this pressure was not painful, and not, I soon realized, physical. It was more like a kind of hum within the skull. I began to experiment with it. I realized it appeared whenever I thought of her with love. Whenever I remembered her, the pressure would come back, sometimes very strongly.

Sitting in one of the watchtowers, I asked her to tell me what this pressure was. Later in the day I opened Aurobindo's *Letters on Yoga* at this:

> In the forehead between the eyes but a little above is the AJNACHAKRA, the center of the inner will, also of the inner vision, the dynamic mind etc. . . . When this center opens and the Force there is active, then there is the opening of a greater will, power of decision formation, effectiveness, beyond what the ordinary mind can achieve.
>
> The center of vision is between the eyebrows in the center of the forehead. When it opens, one gets the inner vision, sees the inner forms and images of things and people from within and not only from outside, develops a power of will that also acts on the inner (yogic) way on things and people. Its opening is often the beginning of the yogic as opposed to the ordinary mental consciousness.

I walked that night to Mr. Reddy's grave and knelt down in the snow and thanked him for having brought me to her.

As I was leaving the churchyard I turned to look once again at the smooth white marble grave and saw the light of the small red lamp Mother had placed there reflected calmly in the headstone. There was no wind that night, only a cold silence in which the flame burned high and calm.

The next afternoon I was too happy to work or concentrate on anything. I went out into the woods and walked in aimless exuberance through the snow. How had I lived all these years and not understood the beauty of fences, or boulders in the stream, or the way sunlight breaks quietly down the green hair of firs?

I felt light as a sparrow, fragile yet indestructible.

And then I saw her.

She was four hundred yards away, with Adilakshmi about fifty yards behind her, standing looking away over a field flooded with light. She was alone, alone with the fields, the firs, the shining snow, with herself. She was walking with her arms lightly outstretched along the frozen ridge of a large rut, her head bent down slightly. I felt the whole landscape was streaming outward from her arms, streaming into them and out along them, like a white heart dilating and expanding eternally, in the same clear moment.

Whenever I suffered or lost heart in the months that followed I remembered her walking along that frozen ridge, calmly, evenly, wrapping the incandescence of winter around her.

I went on into the woods, leaving Ma alone. Adilakshmi had told me that morning that Ma had made a snow Ganesh somewhere in the woods. Ganesh is the elephant god in Hinduism, the god who breaks down all inner obstacles, the god of transcendental wisdom. I decided to find and honor Ma's Ganesh. I wandered up the road several times, and just when

I was about to give up, I saw it. It was about a foot and a half high, a refined and gentle Ganesh, slimmer than most, with eyes as wide and open as Ma's own. It was gazing across to Thalheim as if to fill all its inhabitants with its delicate gaiety.

Ma had left her hand marks on the snow. I found some dry leaves and heaped them in front of it as an offering.

At that moment the snow around me started to emit white light. It was so powerful, I had to sit down. Gazing at the whole white pulsing landscape, I heard her say: *The whole world is white light.*

I understood suddenly why Ma loved snow. Under snow the world becomes what it really is—white, the white light of God. I remembered the light I had seen in Pondicherry, in Mahabalipuram, around her. Her voice came: *This light is in everything.*

I remembered something Ramakrishna had said to a Christian preacher, trying to explain the Hindu conception of an avatar: "Take the case of an ocean. It is a wide and almost infinite expanse of water. But owing to special causes, in special parts of this wide sea, the water becomes congealed into ice.

"Even reduced to ice it can easily be manipulated and put to special uses. An Incarnation is something like that."

*I have made this Ganesh*, I heard her say, *as I have made my own body—to bless the world.*

Returning to my room, I lit a candle before the photograph of Ma that was on the windowsill. It was of her as she had been when I had first met her eight years before in Pondicherry, very young, smiling with tigerish intensity.

I sat in front of the photograph, staring into her eyes. The photograph became alive. It was the first time that had happened to me, although others had described similar experiences. Her face was present, as if behind a veil of quiet light. The light grew, until her whole face was burning in the light.

Her eyes grew larger and more intense. My body filled with the light pouring from them. Everything I looked at—the plant in the windowsill, the book open before me, the tablecloth, the small plastic animals hung on a string above the bed—was shining.

*You will always have this light now when you are concentrated on me and calm*, I heard her voice say inside me, *and through this light I will purify you and fill your mind with knowledge.*

I was being shown, I realized, how I would be "taught" by her. Directly by the action of the Light.

Later that night I talked with Daniel.

"Well, little poet, you are really in for it now. Hold on to your life belt. She's pouring the gasoline into the car. I have the feeling you'll get driven very fast." He rubbed his hands. "I'm going to enjoy this!"

He made me one of his endless collections of teas. "You will be taught in your way as I have been taught in mine. I have not seen Light often. I'm not clairvoyant. My experiences have been of Light entering the head and body.

"This Light can work in a lot of different ways—rather like ordinary light, which is both a wave and a particle, this Light can take on many different forms. God only knows how. I've long since given up questioning *how*. It's enough work just keeping up with what's actually happening. Divine Technology doesn't divulge its secrets easily."

"Although, during the Process you are given what you need to understand what is happening?"

"Sometimes you have to guess a little, or wait. But that makes it all the more exciting. Be prepared for the *plunges*."

"The *plunges*?"

"Well, little poet, I know in a poem everything would go

beautifully and quickly. But real processes are not quite like that. There is a lot of crisscrossing and staggering and sheer error. You make an advance, then you fall back and hit your head on the floor again. You have a run of exquisite, perfect days, and then you repeat all the old rubbish. It takes time to get the hang of it. It's a little like playing a complicated piece of music. You have to practice bits of it at a time, over and over again, with discipline, then slowly put it together and play it all through several hundred times until it becomes as natural to you as breathing in and out, or taking a leak. Ma's is a revolutionary method and works fast. But don't think it is easy. Even if the Divine Light is beaming at you, sometimes you feel, I just can't take any more of this. I want to go out and get drunk. The ego holds on to its pleasures, its silly doomed pleasures, with a tenacity that would be touching if it were not so deadly."

Then he said: "What about a little real music?"

I looked blank.

"You sing. I'll play the guitar. My room is full of equipment longing to be used. Over the years I've made my own small studio up there, and although it isn't quite up to professional standards, it isn't bad. It will be good for you to sing: stop you talking."

That night Daniel's and my musical partnership began. It was only when we were beginning to put our first record together that I remembered the end of the conversation I had had with Ma in my room. I had said, "When I see you looking so joyful and so beautiful, my heart is full and I want to sing." And she had said, lightly I thought, "Sing, then!"

In the four evenings that followed, Daniel and I must have invented nearly twenty songs. They all came effortlessly, without any strain. Both of our hearts were full of her, and we trusted and complemented each other. We were both surprised at the passion, suffering, and joy in the music we found ourselves making.

As I sang, my love for her and my voice became the same thing, the same fire, and through that fusion I began to grasp, intuitively, musically, the kind of gift of sincerity Her Yoga demanded.

Making music in Ma's house brought me to a more refined awareness of the nature of the transformation she was effecting in me. I began to see how the experiences she was giving me had a musical pattern, came in thematic clusters, themes with variations in every dimension from the lowest to the highest pitches. Each of the different planes of my being were strings she could pluck; her grace, and my opening to it, made me able to follow her artistry.

Slowly I realized that Reality lived without the false protection of the ego, lived in her dimension, would be lived as music; that my spirit, when tuned to hers, would, like hers, resonate with everyone and everything in the cosmos at all times.

My first experience of this musical mastery of hers in Reality, and of its meaning, came right at the end of that first stay in her house. It transformed the journey into a dance; it gave me the intuitive key to following her silent teachings. The details are necessarily personal and "biographical": but the experience itself—of the intricate and exquisite interrelatedness of all events and kinds of consciousness—is one that all those who are beginning to awaken have.

Daniel and I were driving back from Cologne, from visiting another disciple of Mother's. This was my first departure from Thalheim in the two extreme weeks I had been there; I felt steeped in clear, deep joy. Everything—the shops, the buildings, the cars—was completely strange, belonging to a world whose existence I had almost forgotten. We drove in a light rain listening to a tape of the early Renaissance composer Josquin des Prez's *Mass of the Blessed Virgin.*

Inspired by the music, I decided then and there to write Ma a poem of gratitude. On a piece of crumpled paper I had in my jacket I wrote:

Rose that never stops
  opening
whose fragrance
fills the cosmos.

Later on I changed the word *fills* to *builds.*

As I made the change I realized, beyond any words or mental formations, the paradox of Divine Power. I realized Ma's extreme gentleness and her extreme power were *the same force.* Her fragrance fills *and builds* the cosmos.

Daniel and I reached Thalheim at about seven-thirty. I felt so shaky and dazzled, I could hardly get out of the car.

An hour later Daniel and I were sitting talking in my room. I had packed for Paris; I was leaving on an early morning flight. Although I knew I would be back soon, I was sad.

A few seconds later the door opened, and Ma and Adilakshmi came in. Ma was wearing a white-and-green sari with a red sweater over it and red shoes. She looked very young and mischievous.

She and Adilakshmi sat down, and for a long moment we were all silent. It was the first time since I knew her that I felt no nervousness, no need to say anything.

Ma turned to me and smiled. At once I remembered the poem I had written. I found it and gave it to her.

Smiling broadly, Ma did not read it but folded it very carefully and placed it on the table in front of her. She turned to her right, to where Adilakshmi was, and pointed past her to the corner of the room.

In the corner there was a red balloon.

I have no idea how it got there. I had been in the room for two weeks and never noticed it.

The silence became bright and hilarious. Ma walked over to the balloon and held in her her hand, turning it from side to side.

As she stood there I remembered the photograph I keep on my desk in my office at Hobart. It is of Ma, staring out, holding a red apple. I had always seen the apple as the cosmos.

Ma walked slowly across the room and threw the balloon to me. As she did so, staring into my eyes, I began to laugh.

She was throwing me the cosmos, the divine awareness, her Light, her Power, and she was throwing it to me as a game, in a play. She was playing with me as a child.

Ma had enacted the poem she did not read; she threw me the rose, the red balloon. In doing so, she completed the series of experiences that had begun in the car with Daniel. She herself with a gesture summed up all the experiences she had given me, in my presence and for me.

All four of us played, laughing, with the balloon. Then Ma put it down.

I went and knelt to her and asked for her blessing. I said, "You have opened my mind and heart. Do not let them close."

She smiled. "They cannot close now."

# FIVE

Returning to Paris, I felt like a child left on his own in a city he had never been to before, compelled to improvise everything afresh. Crossing the street or finding a packet of toothpaste in a store I had shopped in for years became major operations, requiring a surreal amount of control. I seemed to be doing everything in slow motion, like a madman who believes his body is made of glass.

I was not afraid. The body I could hardly maneuver at times was not nervous; in fact, it was calm, so calm it seemed boneless. Once, crossing the Rue du Bac to buy a paper, I had an image of myself as a bundle of loose rags that the wind at any moment could disperse. The thought did not scare me: I realized that I, the witness of the thought (and of the rags), would remain. Arriving at the pavement, I looked at my hands for the first time as if they belonged to something foreign to me, and I felt a kindness toward them, a gratitude for their having stayed connected to me for so long and so uncomplainingly.

After three or four days I realized I would not be able to leave my room. I canceled everything I had to do. My mind, my nervous system as I had known it, was not working anymore. I lived on bananas and vitamin pills. Peeling a banana or disengaging a vitamin pill from its silver casing could take at least five minutes.

Deciding to do nothing and go nowhere released me to surrender to what Ma was doing to me. For about four days, when I wasn't sleeping, I lay on the floor of my apartment in Paris hardly able to move, in a steady, quiet, solid bliss that pinned me like a large moth to the carpet. I hardly felt my body at all, even when I knew that somewhere it was aching. I could not move to eat or turn up the heat. I was lying near the telephone so I could answer calls at first, but after hearing my voice trail off absurdly, I decided to take the phone off the hook. Sometimes, idly, I felt a kind of fear for my body—would it stand being dissolved in this soft fire again and again? But wonder melted all fear. The days became long ragas of light and silence; the music was that silence, pointed up and deepened by different sounds, the traffic outside the front door, or the Brazilian boy practicing tap-dancing in the hall, Scott Joplin from an upstairs window, or the concierge's dog kicking a headless plastic doll around the tiled courtyard below.

I remember very little of those days. What memories I have come from times when the experience was retreating to the fringes of consciousness or allowing the mind to capture a detail, so that it would always remember its tenderness at being eclipsed.

One such memory I would return to often in the months to come was of the end of the whole experience. When I surfaced, I was exhausted. It was a clear February dusk. My room in Paris gives out onto a courtyard; beyond its walls I can see the white wall of another courtyard; above that there is a large expanse of rough wall with great jagged holes in it, where in spring birds make their nests. That evening at about six the wall became alive with a dense cloud of birds. As if at an invisible signal they started to sing together with joy so violent, I gasped. I heard Ma's voice say: *With this wound of beauty I heal your heart.*

I looked at my desk. A copy of Rumi's *Discourses* lay open on it. I walked over and read:

A lion was chasing a deer, and the deer was
fleeing from the lion. There were two beings
in being, one that of the lion and the other
that of the deer. But when the lion caught up
with the deer and the deer, being over-
powered . . . became unconscious and senseless
and collapsed before the lion, in that moment
the being of the lion remained alone, the
being of the deer was effaced and remained no
more.

In the days that followed I did whatever was necessary to be able to return as soon as possible to Ma. A month remained before I had to go back to America to teach the spring term at Hobart. I knew I was in no state to travel, or to communicate, or to deal with the stress of America and the publication in May of my novel, *The Web*. I would have to return to Ma first.

I tried to tell a few friends what had been happening, but I soon saw it was impossible. I did not have the words; the process was not complete. The few times I did attempt to say anything I was met with embarrassed silence. Clearly my friends thought I was mad and were too polite to say so.

I became completely clear on one point: only Love could carry me forward, love for her, love for her work. I continually prayed for that love to take hold of me in the Metro, by the Seine, under the gossip of dinner parties.

After I had bought my plane ticket to Thalheim, I returned to my apartment and opened a copy of Ramakrishna's teachings at this place:

> The young monkey clings to its mother when
> she moves about. The kitten on the other
> hand mews piteously, and the mother grasps it
> by the neck. If the monkey lets go its hold of
> the mother, it falls and is hurt. This is because
> it relies upon its own strength. But the kitten
> runs no such risk, for the mother herself car-
> ries it from place to place. Such is the differ-
> ence between self-reliance and entire
> resignation to the will of God.

Days followed when Ma did with me what she wanted. States of lucid and exquisite inner silence would begin as I was walking to the bakery, sitting drinking coffee with a friend in the Boulevard St.-Germain, washing my socks and underwear, talking to an editor about last-minute changes in my novel over the phone; and I had to learn how to allow them and how to function during them.

I had to learn, in fact, to live two lives—one absorbed in the music she was playing with me, listening acutely to its every shift and stir; the other concentrated on, and responsible to, ordinary reality.

It was hard at the beginning, because just as I had to learn to enter and leave states of trance, so I also had to learn, over again, to do perfectly simple banal things like making coffee or buying groceries. I had to make lists and instructions for myself as if for a slightly retarded child. Well, I used to say to myself, you asked for this change. Now you are getting it. Each change had its amusing side: following instructions in big red letters to make coffee or feeling overtaken by bliss buying shampoo have their hilarities.

After the first days of unreality Paris returned to me, its beauty transformed by what I was beginning to live. Each of my senses was becoming sharper. They way the morning light fell on the rough stones in my courtyard could send me into ecstasy, although I had enjoyed that same view for years. The sight of winter trees against a white sky in the Tuileries made me unable to read the book I had taken out into the gardens. Three Turkish rugs—red and wild yellow—hanging together in a shop window seemed vibrant with Her, and I stood in the rain, wanting to clap my hands and dance at their shameless beauty. The sacredness of every face, every body, made walking in the streets almost intolerably intense—a feast of suffering and loveliness, each face suddenly so near and so poignant. Several times in the Metro I felt myself overtaken by feelings I then realized were coming from a person opposite or behind me. Ma was slowly removing all the screens between me and the world around me, taking away all my ways of protecting myself from its pain and splendor. At any moment a fall of light, a stranger's face, or a Chinese bowl gleaming in the darkness of a shop window could bring me to a halt.

I began to intuit what would be my way of devotion, my way of being always in Her. I remembered Mr. Reddy saying to me once in Kakinada, "Of all the different ways of praying, saying the name of God is the best." And then he had added, "When one mantra is not working for you, not reaching your heart and springing from it, try another. Do not be mechanical about it; always use whatever means move most deeply, bring you most quickly to the place where She is." In those days in Paris I began to say Ma's mantra: OM NAMO BHAGAVATE MATA MEERA (but I always said AMMA for MATA because that simpler Indian word reminded me of my own childhood). Whenever I felt myself relapse into ordinary depression or impatience or casual lonely desire, I would begin again to repeat her name—in buses, going to the post office, watching a film. I prayed for the mantra to become so rooted in me that a part of my being would always be saying it at every moment.

When the mantra of her name no longer worked, I would try the Gayatri mantra, the mantra of the Divine Mother that has been said for millennia in India, or one that had arisen spontaneously in my own prayer, or lines of poems that had shaken me for years, or the slow inner repeating of whole poems that for me have the force of divine speech, such as George Herbert's "Love bade me welcome but my soul drew back/ Guilty of dust and sin." I made no distinction as to where I prayed to her. No place was holier than another. A toilet or a crowded hysterical post office or the cinema were as powerful and happy places to think of her as anywhere else. Because I was scared of losing the rapture she had given me, I was at all moments conscious of her. If five minutes went by without my thinking of her or seeing her face, I became anxious, as if all the joy she had given me would seep out invisible cracks in my skull and never be found again.

As I prayed to her Divine Being, I remembered so many moments of her "human" self—her walking down the stairs sleepily one morning with her hair down, her bending in her blue overalls in the garden, pulling on weeds, her walking in the woods glancing at her watch, her balancing astride the frozen puddle. I realized that there was for her no difference between the moments of what I had to call "splendor"—the moments in which I had seen a small part of her glory—and these "ordinary" moments. Each was infused with the light of Eternity.

I soon found her name written on everything—on the face of the old drunk in the bus, on the newspapers flapping in the dawn street, on the hands of a friend circling a coffee mug, on the shiny black plastic shoes of a punk sitting opposite me, stoned out of his mind, in the Metro. The sublime sonority of the Sanskrit words of her mantra and all the sweetness that broke in me at her name were threads that shone between me and all things, threads that both connected me to all things and pulled them secretly toward my heart.

In that return to Paris I also discovered a friend I had not seen for years, Astrid Delleuze. She is a distinguished and handsome woman in her early seventies, and her directness and spiritual force had drawn me to her from the beginning. But now I found out who Astrid really was. I had known that she had been a disciple of a guru in South India for twenty years, but only when I started to go through my own mystic education did she speak in any depth to me of her own. Neither of us had spoken of our experiences with such candor before. The joy that was born from our conversations sustained us both.

During dinner at her apartment on the Rue de Belle chasse I told her my story.

Astrid smoked several cigarettes, leaning forward in her chair.

When I had finished, she said, "You will have to be very brave, my dear. The process is no joke. It is exhausting. It takes a hell of a toll on the body. Look after your body. You are appallingly thin. Eat properly. There is something extreme about the speed with which you are being taught. I have the feeling you are going to learn in a short space of time what would normally take twenty or thirty years. You are being prepared for the purpose for which you came to this earth."

ॐ I returned to Thalheim on February 13 to find the whole region under a carpet of snow. I wandered in the white hills, stunned with relief at being back.

The next morning Adilakshmi, Daniel, and I were sitting in my room, talking about solitude and spiritual work.

Adilakshmi said, "Ma is absolutely alone."

We fell silent.

Daniel asked, "What can I do for her? What can I give her?"

Adilakshmi said quietly, "Ma lives here from our love for her. It is devotion that keeps her alive. Our love is her food, her bread and air."

What Adilakshmi said disturbed me.

What could I give to Ma; what could I do for her?

I remembered Astrid saying, "You are being prepared . . ." But for what?

I prayed to Ma in *darshan* after *darshan* for the answer. Then late one night a week later the answer came: I could attempt to write a book about what was happening. I could attempt to describe stage by stage, dream by dream, conversation by conversation, the miracle she was unfolding. I had no idea how or whether or not it could be done. But it was one thing I *could* do, if she let me and helped me. I wrote to Ma:

> Please let me try and write about what you are
> giving me, so those who want to can know you
> are here and learn to be with you. I know
> enough to know I am only at the beginning,
> but I know, too, that you can take me any-
> where you want and will, if I am open. Make
> me open. Give me your grace. There is noth-
> ing else I want to do with my life.

I took the letter up to Ma's room and put it under the door. The next morning Adilakshmi came down and said, "Mr.

Reddy always wanted you to be the one who wrote the book on her. Ma says she will give you the Grace."

After Adilakshmi had left, I realized quickly three things: that I would not be able to write anything until the journey—one journey at least—was over; that to take that journey I would have to devote myself completely and in every way to Ma; that from now on the Book and the Process would become inseparable.

That afternoon, Adilakshmi knocked on my door.

"Come quickly. It is Jean-Marc on the phone from Montreal."

I had not spoken to him for eight years, since Mother's visit to Canada in 1979.

The phone was on the floor of Ma's room. I lay on the floor and he and I began to speak with all our old intimacy.

"I am so happy you have come back to her," Jean-Marc said. "I have prayed for this for a long time, you know."

His voice was breaking.

I looked up. Ma was standing above me, looking down. I said to Jean-Marc, looking up at her, "I have come back for good this time. I will never leave her now."

Ma stretched out her right hand to me, and I took it. It was the first and only time Ma has ever touched me, except in *darshan*.

Ma laughed joyfully. Her laughter fell like a sword on the past, cutting it. For that moment nothing existed except her hand resting in mine and the wild dazzling flash of her laughter.

🕉 It was on the weekend following that Ma opened my mind to her "*darshan*." Everything I have seen or learned since unfolded from what I was given in these four miraculous days. I kept as accurate a record as I could.

## FRIDAY *DARSHAN*

The clock struck seven. The door of her room opened. And then it happened.

What happened? I am still not sure how to express it. It was as if a great vibrant humming curtain of molten silence descended. It *did* hum, but *internally*, sometimes near, sometimes far, a great high sound, something in between the supersonic whistle of a bat and the singing of the telegraph wires. I have read enough to know what at last I am hearing: the *Shabd*, the sound of origin, one of the sounds the *Upanishads* mention as announcing the rising of the true, divine Self in the mind.

Mother was dressed in red, the color of Durga, the aspect of the Goddess she incarnated in the doorway in Pondicherry. I hardly look at her as she comes in, sits down, begins. How can she be so small and have so much power, this thunderous power that is filling the room, shaking the room, so strong it takes all my strength to remain standing and not crumple back onto my seat?

I sit down, and the silence grows more and more loud with this hidden buzzing of bees. I feel a throbbing in my breast, round my heart, as if my heart wanted to leap out of my chest.

When I can bear it, I look up at her. She is looking into the eyes of Daniel kneeling before her. Her hands are immobile; her whole body is still as a mountain. She seems for a second or two immensely large, a Kailash, a red, blazing Kailash, exactly the opposite of when she came in. I see her as I saw her in the storm in Kakinada—with the whole cosmos in her body—only this time the body is red, fiery, a burning gold, and it is we who are all in it, the room, everyone in it.

Doesn't everyone see the great blaze of golden light turning around and around her head?

The silence deepens, thickens. Sometimes I lose consciousness in it for a few seconds, and then there is a vastness in my mind full of Light. In that vastness I become Her, the Silence that is Her.

It does not last. The room returns, the people coughing, fidgeting, the man who rolls his eyeballs like someone in a fair.

## SATURDAY

The day is too noisy. Too much talk in the kitchen. Is she or is she not a Master?

I escape again before *darshan* into the woods. There is sanity in the woods, white and clear as the moon that will rise in an hour. Sanity and Silence, that Silence that she will bring down in an hour, intensified to burning point.

The snow is *darshan*. The trees standing silent in the snow are *darshan*. They are as tall as her force, as silent, as dignified, as unanswerable. I think; I will stay out here and not go in and listen to the talk or the coughing or the bodies fidgeting in their chairs. Her laughter and her voice: *Stop this stupid pride. What about my patience with you all these years when you saw and understood so little?*

Seven. Her descent, in white. Again the great vibrant humming curtain of silence. I realize now I will always hear it. She has opened my ears.

Why is the room not in bliss? Why is that man over there picking his nose? These people will drive me mad. Why aren't we in India where people know how to worship? Her voice: *Stop judging. Look to your own worship.*

How much you are showing me; I begin to laugh inwardly. My old rage at imperfection. My impatience. My fear—fear of the ego's ability to betray anything, fear of the endless dreary stupid closedness of this civilization-without-soul. Fear, fear, fear. Stop this fear so I can breathe.

I feel a great wide hatred of everything that does not recognize Her. It is insane this hatred, the exact opposite of every-thing she is. How dare these bastards keep their dull lives intact while I am having mine shattered? I know my hatred is mad. I look at her across from me and see the love in her, the tirelessness, the unshakable patience. I realize that Ma has chosen to work here in Germany, in the West with all the neuroses, despairs, depressions, evasions, gray fears of the West. I realize all this, but I cannot stop the hatred.

*Look at your hatred*, Her silence is saying to me. *Look at where it springs from. Find the humiliation that nourishes it, the fear that continually feeds it, the self-hatred it masks.*

I feel, all at once, the sexual rejections that underlie my ha-tred, the fears of being mocked, of being humiliated for my love of her, of being so opened by her that the world will destroy me. Just as I am about to dissolve into guilt, I feel her catching me inside, stopping me. *Guilt is another pose. Go beyond it.*

At that, sudden reversal. My mind breaks open, and she pours Her Silence into it. Then, her voice: *Watch them; watch these people you pretend to despise as they kneel to me.*

So I watch them as they kneel to her. Each one of them becomes suddenly softer, childlike and vulnerable. Every line in their faces tells its story of weakness or grief or helplessness. Helplessness, especially. The tears come, and with them a great vast steady flame of quiet love that I know is not mine but hers.

As my heart widens the Light around her widens. It is not yesterday's burning, ravening light but softer—the red-gold of the setting sun on the sea at Mahabalipuram. I watch it with my eyes and heart open. It fans out slowly, in steady waves from her, from her arms and head and the folds of her glittering white sari, and slowly everyone in the room is covered with it. The walls start to throb; each head becomes almost entirely this soft red-gold light. My knees and hands are trembling in it. It is as if a quiet wave of light has broken out from her and foamed up over everything.

This time when I look into her eyes, they are softer than I have ever seen them. A thin band of palpable flame surrounds them. I feel as I look into them a kind of film on my eyes *break* and something in my eyes stream out toward hers. As soon as I think to myself My eyes are streaming out, the experience stops. Thought kills everything.

Her voice: *We will try again. Don't worry. Stop judging yourself. You are with me. Let me do it.*

After *darshan* sitting quietly in the kitchen. The ghastly bierstube atmosphere of this morning entirely gone. P, who had said grimly this morning, "Nothing ever happens here," says, "Tonight I felt something."

I go for a long walk. An image comes to me of Ma as an Indian washerwoman beating the dirty sheets of my mind against a rock. She is holding me firmly and will thresh me clean. And then I will lie out on the rocks, unfolded completely to the sun and wind.

Deep in the woods the Silence and the sound, the *Shabd*, return. They are everywhere.

SUNDAY

More snow fell in the night. I look out onto an entirely white world. I am as quiet as the windless snow.

She raises the storms and she takes them away. I remember X saying yesterday, "Sometimes I feel I die and am reborn every *darshan*."

*The darshan of the Mother is also birth.*

I see Jean-Marc in the garden of the Park Guest House in that first summer in Pondicherry before we knew her, reading me a passage from Meister Eckhart's Sermon 7. It is as clear as if I were there. The grass is shaggy in the late-afternoon sun. The white teapot we have been drinking from has over-turned, leaking tea onto the ground.

"Man has a twofold birth: one into the world, one out of

the world. . . . Do you want to know if your child is born, and if he is naked? . . . If you grieve in your heart for anything, even on account of sin, your child is not yet born."

*Each time you kneel to me with real love, the child in you grows a little.*

*Each time you gaze into my gaze without fear, the child in you grows in joy.*

The sun rises in a cloudless washed blue sky. The snow burns radiantly. This evening at *darshan*, silence, complete calm, hardly any thoughts. I hear the words:

*Out of this eternal silence are all things born. You are this silence. Out of you are all things being born eternally.*

After *darshan* I wander in the snow.

I cannot get her eyes out of my mind. They go on staring into mine for hours. I close my eyes in comic desperation. I still see her eyes whether mine are closed or not.

I have walked for three hours in the snow. I am in the same calm delirium as I was when I started, but the body is exhausted. I want, suddenly, to just let it fall flat on its face in the snow and sleep.

At that moment the clouds covering the moon part, and the full moon suddenly burns alone in the sky.

Then, slowly, two dark, thin clouds form around it in the shape of a giant eye. It is Her eye. It is absolutely, unmistakably Her eye, and I am inside Her vast body.

This lasts one second, two seconds, but the knowledge of all barriers between her and me being down for that moment is total.

## MONDAY

I slept deeply until eleven. My body is worn out. My spirit is entirely awake, refreshed. I negotiate the day, leading my body around like a tired old donkey, feeding it, sitting it down, laying it out on the bed when it really cannot do anything else but stretch out.

I am sitting at the window around about four and see Ma and Adilakshmi going out for a walk. I look at Ma carefully in her red cloak, slightly hunched, frowning as she methodically, slowly, crosses the slippery road. She does not look at all like the Goddess burning out in the silence of *darshan*. I feel a sudden friendliness toward her. With all her power she, too, wraps up against the cold, grimaces a little as the wind blows snow into her face, looks cautiously from side to side as she crosses the road.

It is absolutely incomprehensible to the mind, this combination or ordinariness and majesty, supreme power and simplicity, the floppy red cloak and the red-gold sea of light in *darshan*.

She looks up at me and smiles slightly and holds on to her hood that the wind is trying to blow away. Her smile widens.

## DARSHAN

I sit in front of her, unable to take my eyes from her face as the Divine Light blazes around it.

The Light becomes brighter and brighter.

Adilakshmi, who is seated opposite Ma, moves slowly out of the sea of light and bows to Her. In that action she is one with Her. Together they are one long stretch of light.

I look up at Ma.

For the first time I see the great rounded gold shape *behind* her. At first I do not understand what it might be. It is not an aura; it is not the shining of the Light.

Then I realize: It is the shape of the Divine Mother in the paintings Ma has done.

Behind the body of Ma at *darshan* is *that*. It is that that is giving *darshan*.

After *darshan* I stumble into the night. Near the place

where Ma made the statue of Ganesh, I stand and look back over Thalheim.

The moon is still almost full, swimming like a blurred soft goldfish behind clouds. As on the night before the clouds part. The moon this time is not piercing but soft, golden, moist with its own honeyed light.

It soars for one second.

I feel it like a goldfish leaping in my throat.

On Tuesday I plucked up my courage and asked Ma for a time to talk with her.

"Teach me," I stammered, "to ask you the right questions."

Ma nodded.

"What you can say to me depends on how much I understand. I know that." I went on: "Deepen my understanding, Ma. Inspire me."

"Yes," she said. "Come tomorrow at eight o'clock."

That night I had a frightening dream about her, the only dream in all the time I have been with her in which she appeared angry.

We were in my old room in All Souls at Oxford. She was sitting at my mahogany desk, in a yellow sari with her hair streaming down. Yellow is the color of Saraswati, the goddess of music and poetry, whose peacocks had appeared in my childhood, and in my dream in Ma's house during that first visit.

Ma-as-Saraswati looked at me fiercely. *You think I am stupid,* she said. *You think I am stupid, that I do not have a mind. You think that this*—she pointed to the medieval wall—*you think that this has a mind. YOU understand nothing. You are as stupid as they are.*

She was referring, I knew, to the intellectuals and artists among whom I had lived.

I felt helpless to defend myself.

She raged on: *Because I do not speak you think I do not know. Because I do not read you think I do not understand. This stupidity will be your death. This stupidity will be the death of all of you. But why live at all if you do not understand anything?*

"But, Ma," I said, "I know these people know nothing important. That is why I left them years ago. Why are you dragging me back here?"

*Because something of you still lives here, and that part must die now!*

"I want it to die," I started shouting. "Do you think I would be putting myself through all this if I did not want to die?"

*No*, she said. *You want to know more. You want to be even more intelligent and to be able to pretend you understand everything. You are using me to become greater yourself.*

I started to sob angrily.

*But you cannot use me*, she said. *No one can use me.*

"I do not want to use you; I want to be your child. I want to die. Nothing else matters but you. Nothing else matters but your work."

Suddenly she was standing very close to me, her eyes about four inches from mine. She had changed completely and become tender.

*I must be angry*, she said, *so you can be pure. You must know in your whole being who I am.*

I awoke shattered. I realized Ma was right: a part of me I had not dared acknowledge did think she had no mind because she did not speak, chatter, discuss, read.

I had believed I was free of my past and its conditioning. She reminded me I was not free—I possessed those same vulgarities I despised. As long as I retained them, I would be blinded by vanity to the Truth of what she was.

For an hour I felt terror. I tried to pray to her, but I could not.

*I am showing you this pit so you will know it is there. So you will not fall into it.*

The ego is so vast, so cruel, so resourceful . . .
*The ego is nothing. Don't dramatize it.*

Her laughter. *Don't you see I am playing with you? This state of terror also is one of my games.*

Then the fear left. Its departure was as disturbing as its presence. I had believed I was examining my conscience, but she had been making me do it.

ॐ I was still nervous when I went up the stairs to Ma's room. I saw her angry face in my mind as I had seen it in my dream the night before.

Ma opened the door herself, in a red shawl, with a mug of tea in her hand. Her look was full of the most humorous sympathy. She knew—of course she knew—my fear, my awe, my sense of the inability of my mind, any mind, to understand her. Gazing into her quiet eyes and seeing her smile, I knew she had accepted the irony and hilarity of the situation. It was a game for her, another game, and one she played seriously to be of help. She looked at me silently for a while, as if she were gathering me into her through her eyes. Then she turned and went calmly to the chair by the window and sat down. When she looked up at me again, her face had the same playful expression as it had had when she had thrown me the balloon. In front of her on the sideboard there stood the great red bear with I LOVE YOU on it. Adilakshmi had put a peacock feather in its hand.

I began to laugh. Suddenly all three of us were laughing quietly.

"You must forgive me in advance," I said, "for the stupidity of my questions. You know what I feel, don't you, sitting before you after all you have been giving me? Every time I think of saying anything, I feel absurd and want to laugh."

"Laugh, then."

"But what use is language, Ma?"

"Language is useful to make things clear."

"The Buddhists say all talk of God is a finger pointing to the moon. When you have seen the moon, you do not need the finger."

"That is true. But the finger must be straight."

She pointed her finger upward, smiling.

"If the finger is not straight," she said, "then you will look in the wrong direction."

"I know by now you are doing everything," I said. "You have entered every part of my life, and you are opening my whole being to you."

"I was always everywhere in you, but now you are becoming conscious. I am not opening you up to me only but to everything."

She added, "There are others who are also doing divine work."

She was smiling tenderly as if to tell me, Do not exaggerate. The truth is already astonishing enough.

"I have a funny list of questions in front of me," I said, stammering. "Do you mind if I ask them in some sort of order? Otherwise I shall just become drunk and unable to say anything coherent."

Ma pointed to my tea. "You are not drinking your tea. You will need energy." And as she spoke I felt a sudden warmth in my chest.

She looked at me mischievously.

"Ma," I said, clearing my throat, "what is an avatar?"

"What do you think?"

"What do I *think*? If I *think* at all, my mind goes white. *You* know that. *You* make it go white."

She went on looking at me.

"Ma, I can't define to *you* what an avatar is. I feel ridiculous."

She went on looking at me, her smile broadening.

"An avatar," I said, "is God come down in a human body

to do a special work at a special time. An avatar is God appearing in the play of time to bring those in time to Awareness. An avatar is the Eternal acting out in time the truth of Eternity . . ." I stopped, feeling absurd.

"What Ma means, I think," Adilakshmi said gently, "is what you *feel* an avatar is. The definitions of course we know."

Ma was sitting calm and serious now, her hands folded, lying in her lap, quiet, looking down at the floor. For that moment she had the majesty of *darshan*, the great silence.

I turned to her.

"I *know* you are an avatar. Once in *darshan* I saw the world as an ocean of light emanating from you. You are that Sea and a wave of it and all the other waves also. I am not wrong, am I, Ma?"

My voice sounded small and childlike.

She turned to me calmly. "You are not wrong."

We sat in silence.

"You have only asked me one question." Ma smiled.

"What can I do?" I said helplessly, not finishing the sentence.

I began again. "You said, Ma, that there were several divine powers on the earth apart from you."

"There are several. This is a time of crisis. The Divine looks after all its worlds. We have all come to help."

"Each avatar has a different work?"

"Yes."

"But each avatar being the Divine is One with the Divine and all other avatars."

"Yes."

Another silence began, rich and profound. I looked at the next question on my list and laughed.

"You work in silence. This is because silence is the ultimate and final initiation, isn't it?"

"Yes." Ma adjusted the bangle on her right wrist.

"Why is silence powerful?"

"God is silent. Everything comes out of silence. In silence more work can be done. The true experience of Bliss is without words."

The silence returned, this time ringing with her sound.

Adilakshmi came back in with more tea. Ma's and my eyes met. Hers were full of amusement.

"I want," I said, forming my words too carefully, like a drunk man, "to ask you more about this modern age."

Ma held her cup in front of her face and looked over it at me.

"Doesn't your presence and the presence of other avatars on the earth ensure that a new world will be born, that humanity will make a real evolutionary leap?"

"Humanity must work for that leap. Humanity must become conscious. Aspiration is everything. Aspiration and work. My help is always given, my help and my light. But humanity must work."

She put down her mug and smiled.

"Why are you smiling, Ma?"

"Humans want God to do everything. Humans have to do something."

She drew a circle in the air. "One Love flowing around and around. One Love; One Energy; One Mind; One Consciousness." She moved her hand in the air calmly around and around. "Humans must receive."

"Can they?"

"If they want," Ma said, very softly.

"Every day," I began again, "I feel your sacrifice in being here."

"You have your job, no? You are a teacher and a writer. I have my job."

"Being an avatar is a *job*?" I said, smiling.

"Yes. It is one kind of divine life."

"One kind of divine life?"

"Yes. I do what I am told. What God tells me, I do. If God tells me to come down, I come down."

"You have been before?"

"Yes."

"You are not going to tell me when and how?"

"No."

"Have you ever been a human being?"

"No."

The immensity of what Ma was revealing silenced me again. I coughed and cleared my throat.

"Ma, you must be tired."

I was trying to escape. She was giving me everything I could possibly have desired, and I wanted not to know.

"No, no. Go on. I see your list is a long one."

"Like your shopping list at Massa?"

She smiled. "But here the shop is giving everything away free, no?"

Again I felt my chest fill up with her power, an intense warmth that passed as suddenly as it came.

"Ma," I asked her, "if humanity can turn away from destruction and choose God, how long will the transformation you and others are doing take?"

Ma smiled. "How long do you think?"

"Some modern religious visionaries speak as if it will happen immediately, in a flash of lightning."

"No," Ma said, "not like that. It will take time. It goes slowly. Everything has to be made firm."

Again I felt the sudden flood of warmth in my chest.

Her love gave me courage to press her. "You have in this last week opened my eyes to your *darshan*."

She smiled.

"You are pouring light into us when we kneel before you."

"Yes! Different lights for different needs. I see what each one needs and I give it to each. One day you will see these lights."

"With my open eyes?"

"Yes."

"Ma, the gestures of *darshan*—where did you learn them?"

Ma looked at me strongly. "They came. They were there from the beginning."

There was a long pause.

"You must put this in your book," Ma said suddenly. "I am not interested in ashrams. I am not interested in founding a movement for people who do not want to work, who want only to sit around and think about what they think is God. I want people to work. People should go on living their ordinary lives. Family life is a very good place to do my work. It teaches people to be unselfish. I want people to be strong, self-reliant, unselfish, and to contribute to the world with whatever skills and gifts they have. I want them to work—with my light behind them."

Ma began to laugh. "The other day a man came and saw me cleaning the stairs. He was very shocked. He wrote me a letter saying, 'The Mother should not clean the stairs.'"

"He should see you drilling holes in the wall or gardening in midwinter. He'd die or horror."

The telephone started to ring but stopped as soon as Adilakshmi moved toward it.

I looked down at my list of questions.

"One last question . . . Why is it, Ma, that you have no rules?"

Adilakshmi said: "Ma's rules are all inward ones. You find out what they are as you progress."

Ma said: "What use is it *telling* people anything? People must be strong in themselves. What you chose to do for yourself you do lovingly. I know everyone is unique; what is right for one person is wrong for another. I say nothing, but my light changes people inside and helps them discover what *they* want and need for themselves." She looked at me directly. "The important thing is to pray and to receive light. That in itself changes everything."

She closed and opened her hands on her lap, got up quietly, and smiled. The interview was at an end. She gazed deeply into my eyes, and for a moment her eyes were huge and ringed with divine fire.

I raised my hands in prayer to her.

The phone rang again.

Ma put down her mug of tea and went to answer it.

🕉 The next few days were difficult. I was unable to think, work, or meditate; my dreams were violent; I felt trapped and longed to return to a life in my control. My mind attacked everything, mocked everything. I tried to remember all that had happened, all the visions and moments of grace, but the derision continued.

I was afraid. I was soon to return to Paris. Then I would have to go to America and teach for three months. I felt I would now have nothing—neither the old world nor the new. My old life had been smashed beyond repair—but the new life I had been so confident of only two days before now seemed absolutely beyond reach, a chimera, a dangerous silliness. Even if all this were true, I felt I was too weak for the adventure, too conflicted, too broken.

I avoided Ma altogether. I felt ungrateful as well as frightened. After all I had seen and heard, how could I be feeling this? Her calm and beauty angered me.

The pain became extreme. At last I had the sense to pray and ask her inwardly: Why is this happening? What is happening?

No answer I could receive came. My mind sank into darkness. I sat in my room for what must have been twelve hours, too exhausted even to be afraid. Am I dying? I thought. If this is death, I don't care! Get it over and done with.

It was at that moment I looked out the window and saw the snow was falling.

I heard her voice: *My light is like that snow, and it is covering the earth. One day you will see it.*

Her voice was gentle.

*My light is falling over the earth, and slowly everything is blossoming in it. The hardest stones are opening like flowers.*

What has been happening to me? I asked her inwardly.

*I have been showing you your enemy.*

My enemy?

*The one who always kills your hope. The one who believes in nothing. The one who has always wanted to die. But why die now when everything real is beginning? When my light is falling over the earth like this snow? Let the enemy die.*


Daniel next evening: "You have to learn mercy."

"Mercy?"

"You have no mercy. You are very harsh in your judgments. You see yours and other's failings, but you *do not forgive.* You do not forgive yourself, and you do not forgive others."

This is my greatest failing, and I was ashamed that Daniel had seen it so quickly.

He smiled; "Can't keep any secrets from these Slovenian eyes, can you? Don't worry, little brother, I'm a bastard, too. Being unable to forgive people is at least acknowledging their presence; I'd rather they didn't exist at all. Much more convenient. Then I'd be alone with her and my guitar. We're all mad. I've never known anyone who wasn't. Except her. What a joke! The Divine Mother is the only normal person around."

Then he said: "You're starting to see how relentless Ma's force is; she will not relent until we learn what she wants us to. Whenever I want to stop eating, somehow the most delicious pizza materializes. Whenever I wish to control my dislike of someone by avoiding them, somehow I find myself on a long car journey in the rain with them. It is almost comic, this ruthlessness of hers."

As Daniel was talking the memory of a ride in a ghost train I took as a child came back to me.

I must have been eight years old. I remember every detail of that fair—the purple tent with Siamese twins steaming silently in it, the great pink ice rink on which a woman in red tights danced to "Strangers in Paradise." I was intoxicated by the oddness of it all and went back every day.

There was a ghost train at the fair. I avoided it until the last day because I knew it must be as frightening as everything else had been wonderful. On the last day I got into it. As soon as it entered the tunnel, I started screaming. Bloody corpses leered from dark corners; skulls flapped two inches from my face; strange figures—probably beggars hired for a few rupees—walked in the darkness with hideous luminous faces. It was hot in the tunnel, hot with the sultry close heat of a Delhi summer.

Then, suddenly, it was over. The train emerged into a small dusty square with a few trees and a fountain and a row of tea shops. Nothing spectacular. An ordinary, dusty, summer Indian scene. I sobbed with relief to see the sun, the soda bottles, the mangy old dog licking itself, the grizzled resigned faces of the men behind the counter selling sweets or tea. Everything seemed extremely beautiful and precious—the dirt itself, the puddles of dog piss and rain glittering and sparkling like the lapis lazuli of the mosques, like the Taj Mahal in midday light.

In this process with Ma I realize I am in the ghost train again. The fears and horrors of my own self flap out at me, petrifying and depressing me. I must remember they are un-real. I must remember they are my own projections. I must remember they are as frightening and vivid as they are because the "train" is going very fast.

And in the end I will come out into Reality and see it for the first time.

## SUNDAY

The last day. I have no idea who or what I shall be when I return to Paris, to what was once my life, to America. Instead of being scared now, I am curious. I feel like a child on an adventure, as I used to feel traveling India by train, drinking in miracles from the window. She has filled my body with a complete calm. Going to a coffee shop with friends, walking in the snow, talking happily, I feel I am not moving at all, not speaking, not doing anything at all in fact, just resting in her.

Daniel in his room after lunch: "You look six years old today." He brought out a photograph of himself at that age, standing in shorts, warm and melancholy.

I look at him with affection.

"You are the one man I know who has kept his child alive," I said.

"If it had been left up to me, I'd have killed him. But Ma loved him and fed him, and so he survived."

Then his eyes sparkled. "What am I saying? Where is my Western male ego? I did it all myself, myself. I live with her for the view."

He pointed out the window. Daniel's room looks out onto a rough stone wall.

## SUNDAY *DARSHAN*

Heavy snow in the afternoon, so there are only a few people, perhaps thirty. But it is Sunday. No one has been working; faces that were strained on Friday have become quiet. X, who harangued me yesterday, smiles at me. Daniel wanders about, like a great male nurse, adjusting the curtains, making jokes showing off his fresh white socks.

"Who has more beautiful feet?" he boasts. "They are the only part of me that does not need to be transformed."

There are nine red roses in a vase, opening. Their fragrance drifts over the room, rich and heady.

The clock strikes seven. My heart constricts as she comes slowly down the stairs, so small, so frail, wrapped in the same glowing red as the roses. So much fragility and so much power; how will she last her own glory?

A moment later she is seated and seems larger than the room, a heart that is a red mountain. The old woman beside me is suddenly weeping. For weeks her face has been a dull stone; how many lives has she traveled toward these tears? The weeping becomes so great, she has to leave the room. She returns a few minutes later, looking around at everyone with calm astonishment.

The silence deepens and glows with the quiet red fire of Ma's sari, the open roses.

Slowly I feel it happening: I feel her burning away softly another veil between us, another skin. My physical body itself feels the heat and starts to sweat. I look at her. She is completely crystalline, every outline clear, sharp, crisp, as if I were seeing her in the light of the Himalayas and not the slightly furry gold light of the room.

At that moment the veil, the skin, between us breaks. I feel, almost hear it tear open. Ma sits completely still, impassive, as she bends over the head of a young woman. But an overwhelming soft, fiery tenderness has broken all over my being, a fire-water of love that drenches it completely.

*This is what I have been sending you every second for eight-and-a-half years, and now at last it has arrived. This is my love.*

I look over to Daniel. His white socks shine like stars. He opens his eyes, sees me looking at him, smiles his great calm, anarchic smile.

# SIX

Iain in Paris, first evening back: "I don't believe a word you are saying. *Not one word*. But I believe the joy in your face. Whatever she's up to, its saving your life." Then: "This is the only time you've been in love and looked happy."

*From my notebook:*

Three days to America, classes, faculty meetings, publication. I have no idea how I shall cope. I have to write things down on a pad if I am to have any hope of remembering them. "Walk to post office after breakfast; write to X; dinner with Richard (take flowers and Brahms tape); ring agent." But this time I am not frightened; I am exhilarated, for I know a little now of what she is doing.

An image from childhood returns often of a wall in our house that the termites ate from inside. No one ever suspected anything: it looked solid; then one day it just crumbled. She has put inside me her insects of Light, and they are eating me away, and there is nothing I or anyone can do about it. I say her name all day, bless her for being here, understand very little.

Her voice: *I am carrying you in my arms.*

They are like that, these days; I am carried in her body of Light, held against her, moving to her rhythm, leaning against her breast, more half-asleep than awake. My body is limp. Sometimes I rebel and try to walk more strongly or move with the old panache, but I literally *cannot*. The Light will not let me. Daniel would be happy. Always, when we are out walking, he pulls me by the sleeve and says, "*Walk*, not *run*. Why must you do everything as if you have to win?"

Without surrender to Ma and to what she was doing in me, the next months in America would have been impossible. The different states continued—of Light, of ecstasy, of long periods of absolute calm—without any abatement, and I would have been unable to teach or think or write had I not repeatedly said "You do it, Ma; I can do nothing anymore."

I kept these quotes from *The Cloud of Unknowing* over my desk at Hobart: "In a word, let this thing deal with you and lead you as it will. Be the tree; let it be the carpenter. Be the house, and let it be the householder who lives there. Be willing to be blind, and give up all longing to know the why and how, for knowing will be more of a hindrance than a help."

Six weeks into the term I wrote her this letter I never sent:

You are present and vivid at all moments.
Your light floods me as I sit before your picture; you speak to me constantly; you walk in
my dreams.
    I am amazed that I am not always grateful,

that my whole life is not a praise of you. But human love is so small, so self-interested, so afraid of abandon. I, who thought I knew abandon, know now how safe I have always been, how much I have always protected myself.

At first when I returned here to Geneva, New York, to teach, I had no idea what I would do or say in the classroom; I have been teaching for fifteen years here and in Oxford, but I felt a complete novice and a fool. I was afraid also because for months now I have been unable to read or write or think in the old way. I still did not trust you completely. I have read the Hindu scriptures and can trot off all the theories of "letting God do the work," but actually to live that trust is a different matter.

Luckily you made it impossible for me not to.

I had to give up my will to you and let you teach through me. In the first class, about halfway through, I saw your Light everywhere in the classroom behind the heads of all my students. At the same moment you filled me with a love for them all, a love shocking in its power. I realized I had been repressing this love for years, hiding it behind irony or scorn or severity. You made me realize in that moment that I had gone on teaching not to earn money or to "fight for civilization" or any of the grandiose things I had imagined but out of this love of the young and the future. It was not a sentimental love—I saw through it what

I had seen before—the greed in my students'
faces, their fear of work or effort or suffering,
their spoiled consumerist idleness—but I saw
it without fear, and I saw behind it the faces of
their souls. *These are my children,* you were
showing me; *teach them as I have taught you,
with the same patience and love.*

I had no idea how to do this, but I let you
do it. I let you inhibit my sarcasm, bridle my
snobbery, prevent my anger, stop my railing; I
let you uncover in me a new tenderness, your
tenderness, that was working in me. I try to
communicate something of your light. It is
hard, and I often fail. It is hard to teach
George Herbert or Rimbaud to a girl doing
her nails and chewing gum with her mouth
open or a row of boys still drunk from a frat
party the night before—my nerves are frayed
from all the work you are doing in me, and
sometimes I rage in the old way. But as soon
as I do, I feel I have failed you, failed *us,* and
try to save what can be saved.

Sometimes as we are talking, my students
and I, a silence falls, a silence that has a shining of the fire that is You. Of all the many
miracles you have worked in me, it is these
moments of silence shared between thirty or
forty people for which I am most grateful. . . .

I decided to phone Ma instead.
"Ma, you are changing everything."
Laughter, her low, mischievous laughter. "Yes, yes."
"It is exhausting."
More laughter, then "I will help."

*From my notebooks in those weeks:*

The realization Ma wants is complete, of all the parts of the being, body and spirit, heart and mind, as well as the soul. Nothing is to be neglected; every imbalance is checked. The states she sends me are themselves contradictory—to the mind, that is. Sometimes I am full of intense love for everyone and everything, a love so great I know it is not mine, for it bears no resemblance to any emotion I used to feel before; sometimes I am plunged into a calm that no emotion ruffles, for hours, perhaps even a whole day; at other times the tangible world almost dissolves in silence and light; I see nothing but her light, the light that streams more and more constantly from her photograph; at others it is the world that shines with her, vibrates intensely with sweet wild energy. The Absolute has to be known in an many different aspects as possible—personal, impersonal, silent, ecstatic: Ma is turning all the facets of her diamond to me and in me.

At the very moment when I feel I can stand this process no longer, she guides me to a place of balance within myself that I have rarely before found: that balance you feel after a long walk in the mountains, with every muscle singing and the mind full of cool wind.

The only way to keep Her Energy is by prayer, by continual inward prayer, by a turning of the entire being toward the Light. This incessant prayer makes the being flexible enough to take the power poured into it and to make the subtle adjustments necessary to keep it active. Everything at first is experimental, and with every experimental activity there is a great deal of overexcitement, excessively mental formulation, sudden giving up.

Each personality will have a different rhythm, a different way of receiving and containing this Energy, and one will have to work out for oneself how to do it. But though it is hard, it is intriguing. That sounds irreverent; but why be earnest about it all? The thing I have against most mystics is their lack of humor. There are aspects of the process that are very funny. It is funny when the Light arrives and you are in the middle of putting on your underpants. It is funny when you find yourself asking "Please not this afternoon. I have to make some telephone calls and read this book on mysticism." It is funny when J tells me that only scientific criteria for truth are valuable and mystics are pathological cases and I see gold light dancing on his head.

Astrid on the phone: "Talking about energies, what about sex?"

"What about it?"

"For me, thank god, it is no longer a problem. I am seventy, have been married happily, have had three children."

She laughed. "And don't give me the high-minded answer—that you are transmuting sexual into divine desire, that you are living the higher eros and don't think anymore of the lower. There must be a great deal of strain."

"Of course," I said. "But I have decided to be chaste as long as the process lasts. I don't have any energy left over for anyone but her; when desire comes, it masks Her Presence, and I find that more painful than trying not to satisfy it."

"Have you accepted that you may have to leave sex behind to stay with her in the new relation?"

"God, what a question!"

"You will have to ask it."

"I do ask it, endlessly. I don't know the answer. A part of me is willing to give up everything for her. Another part isn't. I was never happy or fulfilled sexually, so something in me clings to an old dream of love. To be an ascetic out of fear, or failure, seems to me contemptible as well as useless; but to have anything but the most authentic sexual love now is impossible. I leave everything up to her. What else can I do?"

"Nothing. In earlier stages of the Path sex is not such a problem. The real Masters, like her, have a very practical attitude to it."

"She has said again and again that it is dangerous to give it up before one is ready."

"But she is taking you slowly to the stage when you may be ready."

"Yes."

"And there is something in your love for her that is your old passion transmuted and offered?"

"She always says, 'There is only one energy,' so, yes, there is, there must be."

There was a silence.

"In the space of clear love there is no problem. Everything is light," Astrid said, "but it is getting there that is the problem."

Another silence.

"She will take you."

"I think she is. I hope I'm not fooling myself."

"If you are,"—Astrid chuckled—"you'll soon find out."

*From my notebook:*

After my conversation with Astrid I found myself wishing I had been happier sexually: if I had, this attempt to move beyond sex would not be so fraught with a sense of loss. Yet I knew that whatever pain and loneliness came with this work with Ma, I simply would have to bear, with as little sentimentality as possible.

This is not her cruelty or her demandingness; the Process I am in has laws I am learning as I go along—laws of concentration, aspiration, clarity—laws as scientific as any theorem and as precise. To rail against those laws or disobey them is simply to obscure the working of her light within me and to prevent the mixing of our spirits and the miracles of vision that are being born from it.

Last night, after a day of turmoil, I realized calmly that I would rather die than fail her, that if I failed her love now, I would find no peace anywhere in anything.

Her voice: *You will not fail me. All this grief is just your old love of drama returning. Be patient. Have I not been with you all this time?*

Soon after I dreamed of Mr. Reddy. I had thought of him repeatedly in this time away from Ma. He was sitting in a large, white, empty room on a cot, younger and slimmer than I had ever known him. It was somewhere in India; the room smelled of incense and fruit.

"So you came to see me," he said. "I've been waiting for you."

"If you look under the cot, there are many pots of food. Ma has cooked it. Fish curry. Very delicious."

He lifted the white fringe of the bedspread. There were seven enormous gleaming gold bowls full of pungent fish curry.

"Go and open the door," he said. "I can't move from the bed. It is not allowed. But you can come and go as you want."

I opened the door. There in a courtyard were rows and rows of people sitting sadly in the heat. No one was talking. All eyes were downcast. There were people of all colors, all nationalities, businessmen, beggars, everyone starving without hope.

"Now," he said, "carry the pots out to them and spill nothing."

I picked up one of the pots. It became extremely heavy.

"But I can't carry it, Mr. Reddy. I'm not strong enough."

He was smiling. "Try again."

This time it was extremely light.

"How did you do that?" I asked him.

"I said her name for you," he said softly.

I walked to the door and turned to smile at him. He was not there. Waking, I heard Mr. Reddy say, "And you still imagine you are living this on your own?"

ॐ Three days later my best friend, Chris, rang and invited himself for the weekend. He had a break in his medical school studies and wanted to spend it with me. I knew Ma was sending him. He and I have been together at Hobart (where I met him as a student eight years before); in Ladakh, where we spent an ecstatic summer immersing ourselves in Tibetan Buddhism; in New York; in Paris. His life and mine had touched and illumined each other at every point. Our quests were intertwined. He had visited Thalheim with his lover and become Ma's devotee.

I tried to tell him on the phone what had been happening. He cut me short.

"Save it for when I'm there. I want to see you and be with you."

ॐ Chris and I sat in my small cabinlike study in Geneva, New York, looking down over the magnolia tree in the garden and its last blossoms lit up by the dusk sun.

"So, what is this Process Ma is putting you through?" Chris asked. "How does it work?" He laughed, "You know me. The mystic scientist. I like things clear."

I explained to Chris, as lucidly as I could, what I had lived to learn so far: that the Divine Mother's Light, through Ma's Presence on the earth, was pouring down into humankind; that this Light would enter anyone who was receptive to it in whatever way it could; that a direct Teaching beyond all images and dogmas and in every dimension of consciousness followed this entry; that the transformation this Teaching then effected was gorgeous and very fast.

"You *see* the Light," I said. "It gives directly everything that is needed—Knowledge, Love, Bliss. It prepares each new stage in the journey and then gives you everything you need to go further. And, once the contact has been made with Ma, it can be received anywhere."

Chris whistled softly.

"What you are describing . . ."—his usually slow and steady voice shook a little—"is a total spiritual revolution."

Chris left.

I was running out of money. I don't earn much from teaching, and I had not been able to do any writing for six months.

The phone rang. A New York magazine asked me to do a travel article for them. I was to submit nine possible places I wanted to write about, and the editor would choose.

I submitted the list. The editor chose the last place I happened to write down—Mahabalipuram.

I did not want to go. I was exhausted from the months of transformation. It was in Mahabalipuram that I had lived the happiest time of the relationship with L, the relationship whose collapse had helped me make up my mind to return to Ma. I had no desire to revisit the place where I had loved L most, at a time when the memory of later humiliations was still raw.

I knew I had to go.

ॐ I phoned Ma and told her that I was worn out, that going back to India was the last thing I wanted to do.

"But you are going, no? You need the money."

At that we both began to laugh.

"I am very frightened. I suffered so much from L."

There was a long silence.

"That suffering will go," she said.

ॐ Term over, I returned to Paris before going to India. "You look different again," Astrid said as I came through her door. "Thin still, but five years older, as if you'd been through a war. It is very strange, this molding of you she is doing. It isn't just the inside she's changing—your look is different. Much calmer—your body, face, everything. Every time we meet these days, I am meeting someone new."

I told Astrid I would be going to Mahabalipuram.

"You thought you were going to have a rest, didn't you?" She laughed. "A quiet three weeks somewhere in the sun, reading Montaigne. I used to believe that. Now for a rest, please, dear Master, a nice dull period with rain and music. But the Process is never like that once it has begun. If Ma is sending you back to Mahabalipuram now, it is because she is preparing for you a new stage. Because of what happened with L, it may well have a great deal of pain in it. You will just have to accept that. If you do, you'll be given the clue to the next part of the journey with Her."

The next morning in a bookshop near Notre Dame, I came across a secondhand copy of De Caussade's marvelous wise work *Abandonment to Divine Providence*. As soon as I read the title I knew I was meant to read it. The book accompanied me throughout the next months.

I opened it and read: "We are really only well taught by the words God addresses especially to us. Neither books nor laborious delvings into history will instruct us about the wisdom of God. They will fill us with a useless muddled kind of knowledge that puffs us up with pride. It is what happens moment by moment that enlightens us."

Her voice: *What awaits you in Mahabalipuram is a death and a birth.*

*Close the book and open it again.*

"If we have abandoned ourselves, there is only one rule for us: the duty of the present moment. The soul is as light as a feather, as fluid as water, as simple as a child and *as lively as a ball responding to all the impulses of grace.*"

I remembered Ma throwing me the red balloon.

I left the bookshop quickly. I sat on the pavement, with my head in my hands.

I have known you all this time, I said inside to her, and I still do not know how to trust you completely.

*Complete trust is enlightenment.*

I walked back unsteadily through a light summer rain to my apartment. I prayed to Ma and opened De Caussade one last time.

"There is never one moment in which I cannot show you how to find whatever you desire. The present moment is always overflowing with immeasurable riches, far more than you are able to hold. Your faith will measure it out to you; as you believe so will you receive."

DOLPHIN
CHILD

# SEVEN

I knew from the moment I stepped off the plane in Madras
that I would be given whatever strength was needed. A wave
of heat swept off the tarmac filled with the smells of my childhood—dung, smoke, sweat, and jasmine (from the hair of the
woman in front of me)—and I heard Ma's voice:

*I have brought you to your true childhood.*

I was home, home in the body of the Mother.

*I am all around you. I am all around you; can't you see me?*

I started to laugh. I am in her body, I said to myself, and
I was afraid. What madness! She was sending me back into the
heart of my childhood, into the heart of its sights, smells, its
intimate bliss, for that was the place where I had first met Her.
In the taxi to Mahabalipuram I saw again in my mind's eye a
film of my childhood I had once seen with my mother and I
dancing and imitating each other on a beach, mirroring each
other's gestures.

*Now you will mirror me.*

*I am giving you back the paradise you thought you lost.*

I gazed out the taxi window, drunk now on each image that
passed by—each cow, each small boy bending in the dirt, each

old woman standing in the doorway of each house, each mar-
zipan—green-and-pink building. The fields igniting in the early
morning sun ignited inside me; the red flowers of the trees
lining the road opened in my mind. Every smell—of gasoline,
sweat, hair oil, incense, dirt, dung, of the slashed leather seats
of the Ambassador I was being driven in—was more intoxi-
cating almost than I could bear. The tousled heads of the two
boys driving me seemed as precious and holy as Ma's own
head. The piercing wild saffron light penetrating everything—
my hands, the windshield, the leaves of the trees—I knew as
Her Light, the Light I had seen burst from her in brilliant
waves at *darshan*. I felt my body, again and again, fall away
from me like sand. What Force reassembled it? What Hand
gathered it together again and filled it each time with deeper
joy?

*You are seeing with my eyes, smelling with my nose, hearing
with my ears.*

The two boys stopped for gas in a village outside Madras,
and I bought a mango and stood by the car in the full sun
eating it, half out of my mind, with the golden juice running
down my chin and chest.

The boys chain-smoked and joked and filled me with wild
pidgin talk about Michael Jackson, illicit booze, the idiocies of
the Tamil Nadu Chief Minister, the tragedies of the war with
Sri Lanka. My conscious mind heard each scattered, absurd
word, but my mind-in-bliss heard only a kind of laughing music,
a stream-sound full of Light, rising out of the heart of the
morning, at one with the car's buzzing and heaving, the landscape's wind and heat.

*One ear, one eye, one mouth.*

*No separation.*

As I got out of the car at Mahabalipuram, at the tumble-
down beach hotel where I have always stayed, I looked at my
watch; it would be nine in Thalheim, the moment when Ma

would be getting up. I had seen her once in the early morning, still in her mauve dressing gown with her dark, rich hair down and her eyes sleepy. She had seemed so young and fragile. And yet it is you, I found myself saying to her inwardly, you who are filling my body and mind and heart with this ecstasy, you whose mouth in mine ate the mango in the sun, you whose ears in mine heard the pidgin hilarities of the boys as divine music, you with your small shoulders and eyes like two brown stars that have this mad power to possess, invade, transform, me at will. Seeing her so fresh and tender that morning I had felt a love for her as if for my own daughter, a quiet passion of protectiveness, the same love that rises in me at the end of *darshan* when, after hours of blessing and majesty, Ma is suddenly alone, small, visibly trembling sometimes with the effort of reassembling the self she uses in the world. How could I be afraid of you, I said inwardly, whom I love so much?

I started to laugh, laugh wildly. I love the Divine Mother, I heard myself singing to myself, in a schoolboy singsong. I know where she lives; I have lived with her; I have seen the whole landscape burn in her body on a balcony; I am burning now, this moment, in her immense sweet fire. I am mad, and saner than I have ever been.

I heard her voice: *Now you are in my right mind.*

The smell of chapati and vegetable curry drifted across the dirt from the circular glass dining room nearby. Suddenly I saw her as she had been on my birthday that afternoon in Pondicherry, going from disciple to disciple, filling their plates.

*Won't you eat something?*

I gazed around the hotel, at the trees in the compound, the deck chairs, the small white concrete huts, the boy asleep by the swimming pool. For one blinding moment I saw only one thing, her, myself.

The two drivers nudged me. "Two hundred rupees only, dear sir. Very special price."

I turned to pay them. Around both of their grinning heads, Her Light was blazing.

Walking to my room, I asked her inwardly, Why did you bring me here?

Her laugh. *So you could be mad with me alone.*

I sat on the sand, laughing. Of course, that was it: In Thalheim I had kept up a normal front. In Paris, also, I had been obliged to play sane. In America I had to get through classes and lectures and faculty meetings. Now I was *home*, alone, surrounded by everything I loved most. I could go mad into Her and dance and play with Her far away from the world, far from all shame or inhibition.

She had known what I had not known myself—that I had needed to live the ecstasy she was filling me with with complete abandon and far from anyone I knew. I had been trying so hard to communicate and translate what had been happening, both to myself and to others. Now I could strip myself of that effort and dive into Her, naked, ignorant of everything but the lucid rapture she was giving me, free as a scraped fish bone of idea and past.

My large white crumbling bare room directly overlooked the beach. I undressed hurriedly and ran into the light and sea. Dancing in the frothy shallows, watching the small sand crabs scurrying after every wave, smelling the fierce, raw smell of the waves as they crashed again and again, I was the child I had been thirty years before.

*The sea is my blood,* I heard Her say, *and the waves crashing softly are my heartbeat.*

I lay on the sand and made my whole being an ear to hear that steady, vast heartbeat. I knew I was lying in her body, the warm wind around me her breath, the water folding over my feet again and again her blood.

I walked home in the dusk, weak with elation, feeling so frail I thought the wind would flatten me against the sand, frail but absolutely clear, washed clean of all pain.

It was at this moment of soaring poise that the memory came back to me of my grandmother on a beach like this being savaged by a stingray.

Oh, no, I said to Ma, don't take me back *there*; not to *that* beach.

Very clearly I saw the late afternoon, the deep-saffron light on the rocks and sand, my aunt sleeping on a towel by my side, my grandmother, beautiful, strong-shouldered, white-haired, wading out in the water in front of me. I heard her scream again, a thin, terrible scream. Shaking, I sat down on the sand.

Why was Ma making me remember this as if it were happening again? I felt, sitting on the sand, exactly the same primitive fear I had felt as a child, hearing my grandmother moan, seeing the great black scar on her leg.

*Open yourself completely to it.*

I found myself weeping, for with the fear of the stingray had surfaced all my pain and rage at L and what had happened here on this beach. The sea foamed around me, and I knew that never again would I feel for anyone what I had felt for L, and that what had happened was not a partial but an absolute loss, irrecoverable, and obscene as the thin scream of my grandmother that afternoon. The wound I had thought healed opened, and the pus of hatred and atrocious anger with which it was filled boiled out in an hour of madness. Alone on the beach, I screamed and howled. But even as I screamed and the howls broke out of me, I was lucid, at once ravaged and calm; the Self, the Spectator, and the destroyed ego, raging and sobbing.

I lived through each treachery, each humiliation of L's and my relationship, each subtle murder on both of our parts. I lived through without any mitigation of pride or self-protection all the horrors I had done and willed in turn, all my desire for revenge. I watched myself again and again stabbing the sand with my hand as if to obliterate L and everything L had revealed to me. I faced what I had never dared to face: that I wanted L dead, wiped off the face of the earth, as crushed and battered as I had been. That desire was as evil as the evil I had suffered.

In that hour I at last understood that I had feared and hated L so much because I *was* him; I saw that everything I had abominated in him, his glibness, perversity, sexual treachery, I abominated in myself, had desired, but been too scared to grasp. He had been my shadow; I now had to accept that, because it was the only way of preserving the love I still felt for him, of rescuing it from the wreck of suffering. I had to accept that because it was part of Her mystery also, the mystery of Her terrible and beautiful work on me.

Then I saw my grandmother in another dark room years later, this time dying of cancer but luminous with her faith. I had asked her why she was so happy when she was so ill. "Because I have said yes," she answered. She who in her life had been so violent and proud had found in the depths of her faith the power to say yes to this illness that was robbing her of her beauty and making her helplessly incontinent. "To say yes with your whole being," she had said, "yes to everything that happens, however horrible, makes you free." About a week later she died, a shriveled, rouged monkey with nothing left of her loveliness or strength. Standing over her dead body, stunned by its sadness, I said to her under my breath, "Could you say yes to this?" and heard her voice, strong and confident, unmistakably in my mind answer "Yes. I said yes and am now free." Now I heard her again tell me: "Every human being has to say in the end what Christ said at Gethsemane: Not my will but *your* will, and when that yes is said the doors of Death and Illusion crumble."

Ma's face swam before me blazing with Light. I began to dance on the sand for her. "Ma, you have said yes. You have said yes to the fools who try to use you, the maniacs who will abuse you and call you a fraud, the disciples who will turn against you, you have said yes to the pain of embodying the Divine, to the horror of dying in a body, to all the torture of absolute love. If I am to be your Child I must say yes also. That is why you have brought me here."

I found myself standing in the sea. The night had fallen. I fell into it and let the waves break over me again and again until I had hardly any breath left.

The greatest bliss I had ever known, indescribable, vast, possessing me in each fiber of my being, each cell, swept me again and again with its fire. Through it I blessed all the humiliations I had suffered. I held them up to the bliss-fire I was and burned them away there, each one, slowly, with a great love toward each one of them. As I did so I knew absolutely what I had previously only half known: that the soul has a power to transform every horror into bliss and that horror is the deepest friend of the soul because it compels it to find this power. It is with this power that the Transformation will be done; it is this power that she is, dying and blazing here, living her absolute yes through every freakish obscenity; it is this power that nothing can break, because it is nothing less than the power of the Divine itself.

"You brought me here . . ."—I started laughing—"to give birth to me. This is birth. This yes is birth." I felt my body fill with the gold of Her Light; I felt my mind break softly open and gather the sea, the waves, the moonlight, the glittering sands, into it; I felt my heartbeat and the waves' crashing become one boundless soft sound gathering and girdling the entire horizon. I was not tired at all, not exhausted, not worn out. I walked slowly, calmly, out to sea.

ॐ For the next week I did not move from my room. I remember little from these days. My "I" dissolved in a long ecstasy that remained unwavering day after day.

I was lucid at all moments, able to answer the door when the boy came with food, able to open and close the windows overlooking the sea, able to shower and go to the toilet. I enjoyed being lucid, too, as a kind of perfect joke. I enjoyed being able to turn on the shower, knowing how to use soap while being completely other and elsewhere. My room had two bats in it and cockroaches; crabs came in from the sand to visit me as I sat for long dazzled hours, not moving, not thinking, immersed in a clear, crystalline sea of soft fire.

I realized when it was over that I had not even thought of her. Not even her face or voice had been in that great soft fiery silence that had completely claimed me, that had become me, or Her-and-Me.

ॐ On the last day of the week, I lived through another hour of horror. I had been sitting all morning looking out at the sea. I wrote later: "There is no word for what this kind of seeing is; I am looking at the sea from within it. All screens between body and thing, sight and object are dissolved, so the sea changing and burning out there is not out there at all but closer to me than my own skin." This is a literal description, but no description could convey the rapture of seeing myself breaking and glittering in a thousand waves before me. All morning this breaking and glittering had gone on in me. Then it descended.

I shall call it death, but even the word is too comforting. What descended was nameless absolute fear—fear that waits at the center, the cobra coiled around immortality.

I have had one trip on LSD in which I thought I would die

of fear, but this fear, experienced with full lucidity, was far greater. It was total. It was not the fear of dying. It was death itself. Each of my cells and senses were steeped in death itself while I was alive and completely lucid.

I watched. I watched how this death stilled the sea, made its every gesture hollow, paper-thin. I watched how it bled the sunlight from the afternoon, leaving only a blurred, eerie half dark behind. I watched my hands blanch slowly and dissolve. I knew what was happening was necessary, and I abandoned myself to it, not knowing at all whether I would or could survive it, or what I would survive it as.

Pure fear is as difficult to describe as pure joy—for the same reason perhaps, that it is completely still, completely silent, an absolute possession. I let myself be possessed by this fear, until nothing but it was left.

Or almost nothing. The Watcher survived, could not be touched. The Witness went on calmly seeing. I became aware that the calm persisted underneath and through the fear.

This awareness, softly, steadily, over the long moments, grew. The fear receded, as if being drawn back into the sea of growing Light that was breaking from some depth in me to which I had never before penetrated. The sea and light and chair and hand and afternoon returned, but beating to the soft rhythm of the inner sea that was breaking inward and outward toward the world.

I realized this deepest and most quiet bliss signaled the end of the experience, and I walked out, still swimming in this state, into the sea. Slowly, with the sea laughing around me, I let my senses return. I felt ancient, and very very young.

During the next days the bliss receded. I began to read again, to read the collected works of Ramana Maharshi. I soon realized one of the reasons Ma had sent me to

Mahabalipuram was to meditate on the Maharshi. I had been born in South India, whose God is Shiva; Mahabalipuram is sacred to Shiva; Ramana Maharshi was considered an incarnation of Shiva and lived all his life on Arunachala, the sacred mountain he worshipped as the god himself. My father, as a young man, had been a police officer in North Arcot, the district where Arunachala is. He had Ramana's *darshan* often; the sage had given him apples.

Meditating on Ramana in Mahabalipuram became a meditation on Ma also. I realized how much they had in common. Both came from humble Indian origins; both taught in silence; both in their worldly personalities were untheatrical, supremely normal; both never sought to defend or proselytize themselves, being sure of who they were. Both had disciples of all races and religions and taught in a way that transcended all dogmas; both, while being Indian and rooted in Indian tradition, transcended their background to address simply the whole world and offer it a way of liberation suited to modern needs. A very tender and personal love for Ramana Maharshi flowered in those silent days by the sea, a love I knew Ma was feeding and opening.

I was being told to go to Tiruvanamalai and thank Ramana Maharshi for the blessing he gave my father and to worship Shiva, in whose country I had been born, reared, and reborn.

I had made friends with a young sculptor in Mahabalipuram, Vijay, and together we set out to Tiruvanamalai on a hired scooter. It took us half a day in the heat and was a hilarious journey because the scooter kept shaking to a halt; neither of us were mechanically skilled, so only grace and guesswork and some random hitting got us through. Moving through the landscape unconfined, with the wind penetrating every bone and hair, with all the smells of India—dung and tea, flowers and dust—constantly washing over me made me feel at one with everything around me.

After about an hour, in a village whose name I have for-

gotten, Vijay halted the scooter by a shabby group of tea shops.
I thought we were stopping for a drink; Vijay pointed to a
large shrine in the distance. "We must not go any further
without worshipping there and asking the Mother's blessing."
It was a shrine to the Mother, to Her power, the Shakti. We
went into the neon-lit shrine with its bored, tooth-picking
priests and herds of young girls walking about in red saris.
None of its standardized cement horror could detract from the
bliss dancing there.

"Do you feel it?" Vijay said softly. "This is a very powerful
place. People come here from all India to beg the Shakti for
what they want."

We stood before a large bowl in which piles of coins had
been placed.

"Do you believe in the Mother?" Vijay asked.

"Yes."

"Then, what will you ask for? Take out a rupee and ask."

"I will ask for our journey to bless us."

"You ask that. I will ask not to go bankrupt. I will ask that
the tourists buy all my Ganeshas." He smiled.

"Do you believe in the Mother?" I asked him.

He looked at me in shock. "I must," he said. "I am such a
lazy boy only the Mother could save me. I like girls and money
too much, and only She could be patient with me. What hope
would I have outside the Mother?"

We traveled on in the afternoon, tentatively, for the scooter
seemed continually on the verge of explosion or heart failure.

At last we came onto an open dusty plain glittering in the
cloudless heat of midafternoon. I looked up fearfully, slightly
to my left.

Arunachala! Arunachala! A great sound like a cry broke in
my brain. I knew it was Arunachala; the whole mountain, the
whole vast rearing pile of rock, was, in that moment, blossoming in fire.

*All matter is this. This endless blossoming of light.*

I saw it in that moment—a great soft shimmering billowing of radiant flame. Matter flaming out of silence, total Silence. Vast Force. Yet the flaming is so soft, soft as breath moving across a mirror, as transparent heat rising in sea wind.

Nothing in the afternoon changed. The other mountains remained impassive. I heard the choked revving of the scooter, smelled Vijay's hair oil and the dust from the road.

I closed my eyes, opened them. Arunachala returned to its calm.

"Thou didst shave clean my head and I was lost to the world, then thou didst show thyself dancing in Transcendent Space, O Arunachala," Ramana had written.

Vijay turned to me, smiling. "You know what the holy men say? Within ten miles of Arunachala all defilements are burned away." He pointed to the milestone behind us. "We have just come within ten miles."

We went to the ashram and found a room. Vijay vanished to see friends after praying at the Maharshi's tomb. I was left alone for two days.

Maharshi had given me the ecstasy of the *darshan* of Arunachala; now he gave me the calm that is greater than ecstasy, that is the abiding in the Self. "It is the ego that deludes itself that there are two selves," he had said to Paul Brunton, "one of which we are conscious now, the person, and the other, the Divine, of which we will one day be conscious. This is false. There is only One Self and it is fully conscious now and ever." In those days of silence near him, the Self shined almost unbroken in me. The days of the descent in Mahabalipuram had been overwhelming; I had hardly been able to move from my chair. The calm I was graced with in the Maharshi's presence was not like this: it was a light, continual thoughtless transparency, calm and pure, with the purity of the small empty room in which his couch still stands, the couch from which he greeted his disciples and on which he died, with the sunlit calm of the morning light on the mountain whose living emanation he was.

I write "was," but the Maharshi is still alive. As with Ramakrishna and his room in Dakshineswar, Francis and Assisi, Christ and Tabka, the place where an enlightened being has been retains always the force of that explosion of Love and Silence.

It was in the last hours of the day that I was brought closest to that part of the mystery of the Maharshi and of Ma that most moves me. I was sitting in the courtyard outside his room reading reminiscences of him. At the end of the book I read the following story: When the Maharshi was dying, his devotees were allowed to file past him for a last look from the Master. One of them who had always been shy and sat at the back in the hall, who had never spoken to the Master, plucked up his courage and threw a small piece of paper onto Maharshi's bed. At once the attendants angrily ran out to bring him back. The Master motioned for the attendants to set the man free and, smiling, opened the piece of paper. On it were written only two words: "Save me." Gazing into the man's eyes, Ramana Maharshi nodded gently once.

I was profoundly moved by the story and for a long time did not quite understand why. I went into the hall to sit under the last great photograph taken of Maharshi as an old man, lying almost naked on his couch, with a look of infinite compassion. Of all the images that survive of him, this, for me, is the most marvelous; the splendid intensity of the earlier face is softened into a gaze of the most refined grace. Looking into his eyes, I understood why the story had moved me: because the Master in it had been as frail as the man looking for salvation, as ultimately worn. Is this not the supreme love—that God can die in a human body, in pain, to bring home to humanity the depth of divine love? Was it not that recognition that had given the man, shy for so many years, the courage to throw his piece of paper to the Master? Finally he had understood something of the greatness of the sacrifice that had been made for him, the nakedness of the Love that had been lived out before his eyes. And the Master had responded with that look and that nod, binding and final as the Law itself.

I thought of Ma and her sacrifice, and I looked again at the photograph.

This time I saw the Maharshi as the Mother; not as Ma but as a man who was also Mother; Shiva, who was also Shakti, male and female at once. He lay on the couch with the openness and fragrance of a woman; age had distended his left breast slightly; the tilt of his beautiful, noble face gave it the tenderness of a mother welcoming her child. I understood why monkeys had come to him to be fed, why children had crawled over the railings around his couch to show him their toys and their picture books. I understood why I loved especially this last image of his Play, for in it he was showing the last perfection, the complete marriage between Wisdom and Love, Male and Female.

Contemplating the Maharshi as the Mother I realized that Ma was teaching me what I must do next, what I must, over many years of surrender, become. I realized that all my sexual and emotional confusion, all the trouble with femininity and masculinity that I had had from myself and others came from a simple inability to understand what I was seeing before me now: that the fusion of male and female in a sacred and radiant Androgyny that is both Father and Mother at once, is the truth of the Divine Nature and so of ours. I realized also that all those years with Ma had made me both more male *and* more female. She had softened and deepened my male will and removed slowly the hysteria and possessiveness from my female power of love. She had given my will its fulfillment and true direction by turning it to her; she had given my passion its home by revealing the hunger for liberation behind it. Her alchemy was beginning to turn me into what I saw before me. The resolution of all my fears and pain over renouncing sexuality was in this image; in its radiance was no renunciation in any sense of giving up or being mutilated; what I recognized in it was the final fusion of sexuality, the place of rest and energy at once, the abandon I had looked for in darker places and with a confused and turbid instinct. In the mystery of loving Ma, the true Man in me would meet the true Woman and their lovemaking at the heart of my spirit would image the eternal lovemaking of Shiva and Shakti, of Silence and Force, of wisdom and compassion, that blissful lovemaking that is the origin of all creation.

I left the hall and walked onto the sacred mountain, up the rocky paths toward the summit of Arunachala. There, kneeling in the sun in a secluded circle of rocks, I did what thousands of pilgrims through the ages have done before me and will do after: I praised the God of Light and asked for liberation in this life, so as to serve God in the body.

ॐ Three days later, back in Mahabalipuram, I had a series of experiences by the grace of Arunachala.

I was sitting alone by a rock on the beach at dusk. Night fell. I watched the sea, rearing and falling, in the moonlight, and listened to that great deep sound of creation and destruction so intently that at moments my whole being rang with it.

Stars appeared, and I closed my eyes to enter the sound of the sea more fully. When I opened them, I saw a great column of white light stretching the length of the sky and passing directly over the Shore Temple, which stood to my right. It was in the shape of a lingam, and the light was as fine and transparent as diamond shavings or the dust of opals. In it, as if laid out on shining silk, was the entire Milky Way.

The lingam blazed briefly and disappeared. I was extremely calm. This, I realized, was a taste of the vast sanity of liberation. My mind was quiet and my body light as balsa wood. Every action—of beginning to walk, of breathing, of shaking out the sand from my sleeves—was done to the rhythm of the sea and the silence behind it. My body was another part of that Body that included the sea, the sand, the stars. One breath united us, one light, one rhythm.

I walked into the Shore Temple and lay along the rock in front of the black lingam and thanked Ma.

As I started to walk back to the hotel along the shore, I heard the sound around me I had often heard when Ma came down the stairs at Thalheim to give *darshan*—a buzzing as if of a thousand bees, very high this time and very insistent. I looked up. The sky, from the right-hand corner, was beginning to peel. I thought of the times as a child when I had steamed stamps off letters; it was as if in front of me the sky was being steamed open. And where the sky had disappeared, there shone a blinding vast white light.

Immediately I knew what would happen. The world would vanish in white light; Shiva was starting to show me His Face, the Face of a thousand thousand suns, as it is written in the *Upanishads*. I knew also, calmly, that I would not survive the experience. I was not strong enough. I cried out:

"Not now, Ma, not now. I want to live."

The experience stopped.

I sat on the sand. I had seen the White Light, the beginnings of the Great Shining, as the yogis call it. Ma had taken me to this point, shown me what lay under the mottled veil of matter, and then put the veil back. So I would continue to work and be alive, but with that Knowledge.

Gratitude for remaining in the body flooded me. I reveled in the sand between my toes, the wind full of the pungent fragrance of the sea, and the nets drying in the boats. I was grateful for each toe and each finger. Everything around me, the boats lying in the darkness, the nets catching the starlight, the waves fanning out in light on the sand, seemed full of calm glory, glory to be worn like a coat, like the coat of many colors of the Hebrew patriarch. I realized I did not want to vanish into the Absolute; I wanted to live here, in this world, with all my senses free and awakened in Her.

Slowly I walked home, and as I walked I heard again what I had first heard eight years before on the same beach—the waves and the wind and the whole moonlit creation singing, again and again, the sacred sound of OM, on and on, a thousand thousand intermingling OMs, loud, soft, high, low, stretching like the lightning on that afternoon in Kakinada from one end of the horizon to the other.

The next day I went to meet Vijay at his shop on Rathas Road.

"I asked the Maharshi not to be bankrupt and see . . ."— he brandished a letter—"today my brother-in-law says he will support my business. Today I am full of belief in God."

He grabbed my arm. "Let us celebrate. I will take you to see my favorite sculptures. I will teach you everything about sculpture!"

We walked the length and breadth of Mahabalipuram, Vijay talking exhilaratedly, I listening. As the sun set we found ourselves standing in the last group of temples.

"Now I will really show you something," Vijay said, forgetting I had been there many times. "You must close your eyes."

He put his hands over my eyes and led me around the temple to the other side. "Now open."

In front of me, lit up by the late sun, in its niche of gold stone stood a statue of Siva Ardhanarisvara, that aspect of Shiva that is half Shiva and half Parvati. I had always loved the statue, but today it was as if I were seeing it for the first time, brimming and opulent in the dusk.

"You see," Vijay was saying, "the left side is Parvati, is Shakti; the right side is Shiva. Look at the beautiful breast." Vijay sighed. "Only European girls have such beautiful breasts, but they are so cold. Look how even in the face there is both male and female. The left side is softer, sweeter, like a German girl I saw . . ."

He went on. I hardly heard him. My body was filled with ecstasy. Vijay stopped and wanted to go on. I asked him, shaking slightly, to leave me here in front of the statue.

"I will meet you by the rock on the beach later," he said, "and I will take you to dinner. Today I am a rich man."

He left me alone with the statue.

I realized all the experiences in Mahabalipuram and Tiru-vanamalai had led up to this moment and the recognitions it engendered.

Years before, my friend Chris and I had been in the Met-ropolitan Museum in New York and had walked by chance into the Polynesian section. There we had seen two majestic straw figures, with the ritual titles "Lord-Mothers." We had been talking about Whitman. "Whitman was a Lord-Mother," Chris had said, adding, "and that is what we must become." It had been one of the epiphanies of our relationship, one to whose mystery I had often returned.

Standing before the statue, I realized Ma was slowly making a small Lord-Mother out of me. It was the Lord-Mother that I loved so much in the Maharshi; in Tiruvanamalai I had wor-shipped him, I saw, as Siva Ardhanarisvara.

The statue glowed in the sunlight, smiling.

Then I realized also that the fusion of "Lord" and "Mother" in the spirt leads to a state comprehending but transcending both. The marriage of opposites engenders the Child, free of all dualities, because it is master of them, free to play.

I saw Mr. Reddy's face shining briefly in the air. I saw I was being given the secret and symbol of my life and journey with Her.

A late gold-red light flooded the niche where the statue stood.

A memory swept me of standing years before on a rock in Santoríni and seeing a dolphin leap in the sun on the horizon.

The words came: *The child is a dolphin in the sea of light that is my creation. The whole sea is its home.*

I found myself repeating: "Lord-Mother, dolphin-child. The Lord-Mother is my dolphin-child."

Slowly the golden light left the statue. I knelt to it.

"Ma," I prayed, "make me become what I have seen."

Vijay was sitting on a rock, smoking a cigarette, gazing out to sea.

"So you saw it, did you?" he said.

Something in his tone alerted me.

"Saw what?"

Vijay threw the cigarette away onto the sand and buried it with his heel. He came over to me and put his hands on my shoulders.

"Look around. What do you see?"

"I see the Shore Temple. I see the sea and sand and the late sunlight on both."

"Sea and sand," he said quietly. "Shakti and Shiva. The Shore Temple. Shiva and Shakti."

"So now you know!" Vijay was looking at me amusedly.

The afternoon had so shaken me, I could not follow him. He explained.

"This place is a sacred place. That you know. You come back year after year. It is sacred because Shiva has been worshipped here for thousands of years, because the gold stone from which the sculptures are carved they say is the color of the Divine Ananda, the bliss of God. It is sacred because all things are here together, sea and sand, wind and light. All opposites are here combined. Look at the rock: it is solid, but in the light of morning it looks like golden water. Look at where we are—on sand, but only a few feet away from the sea. Look at the Shore Temple, at once delicate as a woman's fan and strong, Shiva and Parvati in one building, Shiva's strength and Parvati's delicacy dancing together in stone." He looked at me.

"Why I took you to the statue of Siva Ardhanarisvara at the end of this day was because *that* is the god of this place. It took me many years to understand this. I love you as a brother, so I gave you this."

He smiled. "You see, dear friend, I do not think only about money and girls."

I realized as Vijay was speaking that Ma was speaking to me through him, revealing at last details of a pattern that had brought me again and again to Mahabalipuram. I gazed around at the sand turning a passionate crimson in the final rays of the sun; at the sea, quiet today, breaking in fan after fan of foam on the shore. All the visions the place had given me returned to me, and I sat on the sand feeling its still warmth rise up through my body.

I could not speak for a long time.

Vijay sat with me, smoking and smiling to himself.

I broke the silence as evening was falling.

"You said,"—I turned to him—"that the gold rock from which the sculptures here are carved is the color of the Divine Ananda."

"Yes," he interrupted me. "Don't you see? How many times have you been and still you do not see?"

He was mocking me, playfully punching my arm.

"So you want me to reveal everything and *still* buy you dinner?"

"Yes."

"You want everything, don't you? I like this. I also want everything."

He sat silently for a few moments. "I have been lucky in my life. I have not had money, but I have had great teachers. My sculpture guru was a great man. He lived all his life here. He knew everything about sculpture and knew all the sculptures by heart. For him making a statue and worshipping God was the same thing.

"One day, after I had been with him three years, he took me to lunch at the Mamalla Bhavan, you know, the place in the center of town. Very expensive lunch. Seven rupees. 'Eat as much as you like,' he said, 'because today is a good day.' I did not know what he was talking about, but I ate like an American, many, many helpings. Then he took me outside, to a place on the rock in the shade, where we slept. At about five o'clock, when the sun's glare was beginning to go, he took me to the great Ganges rock and stood me in front of it.

" 'What do you see?' he said. I thought, Has he gone mad? I know every inch of this sculpture. I have copied the snakes and monkeys for him; I have spent mornings following with my eye every detail of the elephant's body, of the limbs of the gods waving from their rock heaven.

" 'What do you see?' he repeated. I carefully retold the story of the sculpture, of how the Ganges had descended on earth from Shiva's hair because of the great penance of a yogi. And how that descent had made the whole of nature happy. I named the animals and yogis and gods one by one.

" 'What do you see?' he repeated.

" 'I have told you.'

" 'You have told me nothing. Any tourist on bhang could

tell me what you have told me.' Then he smiled. 'I will tell you now something I only tell the students I love. Keep it always in your heart.' "

Vijay now stood up.

"I wish I could bring him back here for you. He was a very thin man with spectacles that were broken and stuck together with cellotape. He stooped a little. He had a long, thin nose like a Kashmiri and eyes soft as a young girl's.

"He said to me, standing straight for once, very straight, 'Once as a young man not much older than you I was praying in the evening in the Shore Temple. I was sitting in the room of Shiva and Parvati facing the sea. The light from the sea filled the room. Suddenly I saw a figure standing in the light. It was Siva Ardhanarisvara. One side of his body was clothed in gold and purple; the other was naked except for a small red cloth wound around his middle. I could not see his face, but I saw one hand raised in blessing. I was not afraid. I gazed into the light and many things were communicated to me silently.'

"He pointed to the rock sculpture of the Ganges. 'The men who sculpted this for the Pallava kings were not mere sculptors, they were holy men, inspired by Shiva himself. And what they were sculpting in the gold rock, in the rock that is the color of the Divine Ananda, is that Ananda in creation, is creation itself flooded by Ananda. The beauty of the gods that you see, with their perfect shining bodies, their smiles, their hands raised in greeting and blessing, is the true beauty of human beings also, their hidden beauty. The happiness and love of the animals is their true happiness. What the sculptors all those years ago have done for us is to give us in solid form a vision of the Divine Life on earth, of the earth as one day it will be— and to the illumined already is—opened like a full lotus in the sunlight of God's Love.' "

Vijay fell silent. It was evening. A cool, fresh wind was blowing from the sea. The first stars were glittering.

Vijay smiled. "And now we must eat. All this joy is making me very hungry."

I tried to stand up and tottered.

Vijay caught me before I fell. "Put your arm around my shoulders," he said. "We'll walk like two drunkards."

The moon above us was almost full.

# EIGHT

Two weeks later I got out of a taxi in the middle of a gray afternoon in Thalheim. Ma was standing outside her house in her gardening clothes. It was astonishing after all I had been through with her in the last months to see her, so small and natural, with her hair down. She nodded once and went on with her work.

The following days were long, warm, and silent. I tried to begin my book on her but abandoned it. The vastness of what Ma had given me in Mahabalipuram had stunned my mind quiet.

I let the bliss Ma was sending me find me. I offered myself to it and let it open my veins and dance in my brain and possess my body. I spent days on end walking alone in the hills, exploring new paths through the woods. Each day my love for the landscape in summer deepened, and I saw her in its glowing abundance more and more unmistakably—in the flowers pouring themselves from the hedgerows, in the thousands of fresh green leaves turning in the sun, in the sweet, musky curve of the low hills, in the wheat, buzzing with insects, thick with golden life.

The smallest rain-damaged rose would silence me; a horse streaking across a field would fill me with such joy I had to sit down; the streams in the woods did nothing but whisper her name in syllables of water-light.

At night I would go up to the wheat field on the hill above Thalheim and watch the moon come up over it. The ancient German tribes had worshipped the Mother in the fields like this, and I found Her still there—immense, diaphanous, intact.

Ma was taking me into a new stage, into her house of Unity, that inner state in which the whole creation is perceived as one thing, and one thing only. I moved and breathed and the summer moved and breathed and glittered around me; I sat on a bench, and the wind in the leaves and my gesture of sitting were part of the One Gesture that repeated itself with infinite subtle and delicate variations through the whispering branches and swaying grasses, in the birds diving and swooping over the green fields, in the rabbits leaping suddenly out of their hiding places, in the flapping of my green trousers in the wind. I walked under the trees and knew that my walking beneath them was part of their lives also, for their sympathy and patience communicated themselves to me in my silence and found me out and sustained me.

Late one afternoon about ten days after I had arrived, I knelt to her in a clearing and said inwardly: You have brought me here; I am here at last; I have arrived on earth; I know now that the creation is rooted in bliss. As I knelt, a wave of brazen power swept my body and mind, and I heard from all the trees and grasses and hidden animals around me a soft cry of welcome, of blessing.

Her voice: *From now on this bliss will never leave you. You have come into my kingdom.*

🕉 I waited two weeks before I asked Ma for another interview. I wanted to be as clear, as tuned to her, as possible. Sitting with her on the safa in her room, with a mug of tea in my hand and the afternoon sun pouring in through all the opened windows, I burst out laughing.

"Oh, Ma," I said, "here you are in your gardening clothes, and I know now that you are dancing in light everywhere and that you can do anything and be anything you want."

Ma turned to me, her face suddenly still and blazing. Her face became the Face of the Goddess.

I could not speak for a long time. I looked around at the room, at the striped wallpaper, at the plants on the windowsill, at her, so still and so beautiful.

"When I was in Mahabalipuram," I began softly, "I had visions of Shiva, but Shiva is in you. In the 'Devi Mahatmyam' it says that all the lights of all the gods are in the Light of the Divine Mother."

"This is true."

"The Divine Mother then can teach her child through any of the religions, any of the gods, any holy teacher."

"Yes."

"Ramakrishna said that the Divine Mother cooks for each child what food he or she needs. Some like plain white fish; some like it curried."

"And some," Ma said, "like it with lots of potatoes and oil, like Daniel." She said that with such love for Daniel that all my love for him also went through me.

The sound of traffic drifted through the open windows.

"If I had gone to Rome and was Christian, then you would have taught me through Christ?"

"Yes."

"You have come to give the Light to all people, so all can awaken in whatever way they choose, in whatever situation or society or religious discipline they find themselves."

"Yes."

"You provide the electricity, and the different lamps light up."

Ma laughed. "Yes. Light is the best electricity. *Total* electricity."

You do not want disciples in the old sense."

"No. If people want to come to me, I can give them the Light. If they want to be taught by me inwardly, I will teach them. If they want to take my Light and be taught by someone else, they can."

"Daniel said a beautiful thing yesterday," I went on. "He said you never treat any of our visions of you or the Light as special, because you never want us to rest at any stage or state."

"Yes," Ma said. "There is always more. Always. Even for the greatest of yogis, even for Sri Aurobindo, there is always more. You must go on and on aspiring, praying for more and more Light."

"Realization is not, you have been showing me, one marvelous moment. It is a Process."

"Yes. A journey without end. There are different stages in the journey, but the journey has no end."

"The great danger for me," I said, "is that the ego will seize what the soul is learning for itself, to make itself proud."

Ma laughed. "It will try. But the soul's joy will break it down, no?"

The silence returned, humming and vibrant.

She fixed her eyes on me. "The Divine will not use you unless you are humble. My power passes through those who are clear. Keep yourself clear at all times."

A cloud blocked the sunlight, darkening the room for a moment, then it passed.

"Many people now believe," I said, "that the evil powers are in control."

"They are not in control. The Divine is in control. The Divine knows how to use evil."

"Evil imagines it is intelligent."

"Intelligent? Evil is stupid. It understands nothing. It understands only greed, only cruelty."

"Evil is stupid because it thinks only of itself."

"Yes. Only the Divine knows what to do and how to do it, because the Divine thinks of all things at once."

"How do you convince people of this?"

"Live your life for God, and they will be convinced. Only actions convince."

"How do you convince people at a time like this that they can do anything? Nearly everyone I know feels overwhelmed by the extent of the danger to the world, overwhelmed and cynical and afraid."

"The Divine is here," Ma said strongly. "The Light is here. I am bringing down the Light. Others are working here with me. People must know that and know that the Light will help them and make them strong. They must know that, if they work with the Light, it will transform them and give them the power to change themselves and so change the world. Everyone has a great responsibility now to work to change the world. This is a very dangerous time." She paused. "But it is also a great time, because the Light is here and people can aspire to it."

"But the power and force of evil are terrifying."

"Stop being afraid." She had raised her voice slightly. "Root yourself in the Light." She pointed to the plants in the windowsill. "Live on the Light like those plants live in their earth. Make the Light your earth, your food, your strength, and nothing can destroy you."

"Has the evil of this century happened to make humanity aware of the madness of living without God?"

"Yes."

"So humans can turn to God now and take the leap into another Being that God is preparing for them?"

"Yes. This leap is certain. It will happen. It is happening now."

"The old world will fight to keep its power."

"It will lose," she said, smiling.

I watched Ma, smiling quietly to herself, leaning forward in her chair. The Light was streaming from her hair.

She raised her tea to her lips, and the vision ended. Our talk was over. I stammered my thanks and got up to go. Her eyes followed mine to the door, to steady me.


The next afternoon I opened the glass door that leads into the garden and saw Ma sitting on a small square stone in the middle of the flower bed.

She looked up quietly, her eyes feeding mine with peace, then returned to weeding.

I felt I should leave her alone, but I heard her voice inside: *Stay in my garden with me.*

I sat on the bench and watched her. A late-afternoon sun fell on the garden. A warm wind filled it with the fragrance of fresh grass.

I heard her voice say: *I will always be here in the garden of your soul. No force in hell or heaven can shake that now.*

The Mother without was the Mother within; the garden radiant in the late-summer light was the soul's garden; this silence that was deepening in my mind was the same silence that infused and underlaid and sustained every created thing.

*No separation. No walls. Only one thing.*

She carried on weeding, the Light streaming from her hands, her face, her hair, the mud-splashed red shoes she was wearing.

She looked up and saw I was looking at her.

"All the worlds are here," I said. "Thalheim is heaven; heaven is here."

"Not just here," she said. "Everywhere."

. . .

Three days later, after *darshan*, I left the room and went into the garden. The order seemed to come from her. It was a cloudless pale-blue summer evening.

I sat where I had sat before, and the same bliss entered me. Then I looked up. All around me, pouring down from the sky on the garden, on the roofs of the surrounding houses, was an intense fine white light, a soft flaky blizzard of slightly pearly white light. I knew this was the Paramatman Light, the light of the Absolute, Ma was bringing down onto the earth. It was falling everywhere—on the hands I outstretched to it, on the dirty grass, on my shoes, on the apples—an endless, calm, unstoppable, radiant fall of Light falling on everything, penetrating everything. I was seeing it with open eyes, at all moments aware of my surroundings, the birds on the telegraph wire before me, the feel of the moist summer grass beneath me. The Light fell most intensely around the uncarved square stone Ma had sat on. The red plastic gloves Ma had used to weed lay by the stone.

I studied the apple tree I had gazed at before. It was leaping in stillness to receive the Light. It seemed, in that brilliant silence, to be flinging open all the pores and cells of its being to the Light that poured into it.

I prayed for the ardor of the fruit tree, the passive rapture of the long grasses, the patient infinite receptivity of the stone walls that also pulsed and shivered with love of the Light.

Laying down on the steps of the house, I viewed the sky, which was melting into a quiet light violet. On the horizon two vast long, thin irradiated pink clouds were converging slowly to meet each other across the windless mirror of the evening.

I became the two clouds moving. They were moving not without but within me, within the vast outflung airiness of my new consciousness. I was, for those moments, the whole sky—

the houses, the hills, and the clouds moving in rapture across the fine quivering membrane of violet light within me that was the sky.

Then the clouds met, there, on the horizon and here, inside the Heart, and the immense tenderness of their meeting, like two air whales meeting in that violet ocean of light to make love to each other, exploded along the veins of my body and mind.

🕉 On the next morning I went up to Ma's room. She was sitting, eating her morning toast.

I explained what I had seen.

"Did I see the Paramatman Light?"

"Yes."

I described what I had experienced on the steps.

"This is your normal consciousness, isn't it?"

"Yes," she said.

"The Light is entering everything, everything," I stammered. Ma went on eating.

🕉 Two days later I was in Frankfurt station on my way to Florence to work on a journalistic assignment. Waiting for my train, I browsed in the station's bookshop. I had no desire to buy any of the newspapers and magazines but knew by the gathering pressure in my body and forehead that I was being led to something. I was about to leave when I saw the August edition of *GEO* staring at me. I reached for it mechanically and found myself paying for it and taking it out into the station.

I opened the issue at random and gasped. There, in front

of me, was a photograph of the Andromeda supernova, the same image I had seen years before in front of me at Aurobindo's tomb.

I gazed at the photograph and then at the article it was illustrating. The article was on spirals. Immediately there flashed before my inner eye a vision of a vast endless starlit darkness in which a huge spiral of Light, larger by far than the Milky Way, was rising. The darkness and the spiral were not separate: both fed from and sustained the other.

Messages arrived:

*Evolution is a spiral.*

*What you have lived with me is a spiral.*

*Yoga is a spiral.*

*Time is a spiral within eternity.*

Phrases from the article leapt up at me: "Spiral growth makes optimum the dances of life"; "forces working on each other create spirals"; "many leaves form themselves in spirals to use the light as well as possible."

I studied the photographs of all the various forms of spirals in nature—in the dance of electrons, in the filigree shapes of water left in sand, in the Christmas tree form—and again and again I heard Ma's voice.

*What I am doing spirals from the heart of nature.*

*And there is no difference between the transformation of matter and the transformation of the mind.*

*One energy: one spiral: one transformation.*

I realized the illumined and aspiring mind of humankind will be what channels the Force of the Mother, the Shakti, which is descending in the Light. The mind will channel the Force, and the body will dance in it, and the whole being of humanity will ascend slowly, inexorably, to a new identity, a new power.

I realized as the train raced toward Florence that the vision I was being given would also be shown in different ways to thousands, perhaps millions, of people all over the world. The new creation is announcing itself in all cultures, in all the religious traditions of the world, in the dreams of ordinary people, in visions, in new works of art.

I heard her say:

*Now I will show you the twentieth century.*

*Gaze with all your courage into its darkness.*

I saw writhing bodies, burning, flayed, spattered with blood. I saw bombs flowering, the faces of mad dictators as they cut open the eyes of living children, torturers masturbating over the women they had just electrocuted. I saw all these nightmares arising out of the darkness and returning to it.

Then, just as I thought I would faint because I could not bear the sight and smell of so much horror, I realized, with a clarity and certainty beyond my power to express, that this terrible, unparalleled filth and depravity, this unspeakable desolation spread out over every continent and enacted in every culture, was feeding the New Light.

*The spiral of light rises out of the darkness.*

She had come because the cries of the tortured and mutilated had called her; She was here because a million tears and screams had pulled her to her torn and battered creation. The horror that humankind had revealed to itself had driven it to call for a new hope, a new world. The depth of that cry was answered, I saw, by a force, a passion, a height of Divine Light that sprang directly out of the heart of the horror, that flamed out, invincible, from its center.

As these revelations came to me, the vast spiral of Light started to twist and turn into all the colors of the spectrum. In the middle of this whirlwind of Light Ma appeared, in a white sari, smiling as if in her room at Thalheim. The spiral shrank and became a luminous snake she wore around her, a diamond snake. And then she stood, once again, as in the doorway in Pondicherry that evening surrounded by white light, when she had turned to me and smiled her smile of triumph.

🕉 I returned from Italy to a Thalheim celebrating summer with kermess. A huge red-and-yellow tent with allegorical paintings of the various regions of Germany on it had been erected in the crossroads above Ma's house. The local boys lolled nervously at the soft-drink stands or promenaded their motorbikes ostentatiously up and down the road. It was strange after the months of silence to have the village full of normal suburban merrymaking. One of the more puritanical disciples spoke coldly of the fair to Ma. She said, "Why shouldn't people be happy?" Twice I dreamed of her in the next days riding on one of the merry-go-round's red-and-blue horses.

Three mornings after I returned I asked for an interview. It was fixed for the late afternoon.

At six Ma met me at the door, dressed in a red-and-gold sari with hand-painted red flowers on it.

We sat together on the sofa. Ma's hair was loose, falling, richly scented, down her back.

"You are so beautiful today," I said. "The whole summer is burning in you."

She turned and looked up at me. Her face became still and shining, and we sat together, looking calmly at each other.

In the silence that followed all the questions I had wanted to ask slipped from me. Adilakshmi came in, and the three of us sat in peace.

"All this summer," I began, "you have been drawing me into your Heart, into your Unity. I am starting to see that you have always been the same. I have been moving. You have always been still."

Ma murmured softly, "I never change. The body changes, gets older. But I never change."

Adilakshmi said, "Ma is everything. This peace we feel is the peace from which all things rise and into which all things fall." Neither of us could say anything for several long moments. Ma sat, looking down.

"When I am one with you," I began again, "we will not need to talk anymore."

Ma nodded.

"But for now," she said, smiling, "you are allowed to talk."

"Yes," I said. "I crawl across your desert of silence toward you, with every real question coming a little nearer." She looked down, still smiling.

I told Ma everything that had happened in the train to Florence.

"Sometimes when I am receiving you I think I am crazy."

She laughed. "No, you are not crazy."

"The Divine is a spiral, and that spiral takes the human up with it."

Ma laughed and made the action of a double spiral in the air with two hands.

"Everything I have lived and seen and known with you, you have been orchestrating. I have only been receiving."

"But receiving is a great work, no? To be clear is hard. You are becoming clear."

At that moment rays of vibrant sunlight entered the room from all its windows. I laughed out loud and clapped my hands.

Ma looked at me amusedly.

"Everything with you mirrors everything else," I stammered. "What is outside dances around what is in you."

"There is no difference between inside and outside. Everything outside is inside. As you awaken, the whole world appears in your heart."

Silence filled the room.

"Talking to you," I said after a while, "is like playing music. There are themes that come back again and again in a different way, and there are long silences full of the sounds of what has been played."

"You are playing and listening," Ma said.

"I am understanding, too, that how I learn to play with you in this room is how I learn to play in the world and with the world. If I can be open to you entirely, I can be open to the world. There is no difference."

"No difference."

"In the end you and I and Reality will be One."

"One music. Always changing and always the same."

"You will be playing me."

"I will be always tuning you, and you will always be letting me tune you."

Sunlight surrounded Ma, lighting up her face, her hands, her lap.

Tears came to my eyes.

"It is hard for a human being to come naked into your world."

"But you are not naked. I have given you my Light. You can wear that."

Ma rose and went to stand by the window.

She turned, gazed at me with infinite kindness, and again a peace fell on the room. In that peace all my feelings and visions and thoughts and meditations, all the experiences of the last months combined and gave me the strength to say to her: "I know who you are, Ma. You are the Force that can unify the world. You are the Force that is creating the new evolution. You have come down to us as a tender, simple Indian girl, so no one can be afraid of you. You speak in the universal language of love and silence, so what you say can pierce all dogmas, all cultural differences, all laws."

I knelt down on the carpet.

"I am here," Ma said. "Those who want to see can see. Everything that can be done to open the mind of the world is being done."

I gazed up at her, standing there alone and majestic against the window. The Divine Light was streaming from her face, her hands, her hair.

The telephone rang.

Ma shrugged her shoulders lightly, deliciously. The interview was over.

Late that afternoon I listened to Thomas Tallis's *Spem in Alium*. It is a motet written in the sixteenth century for forty voices, forty separate parts. I first heard it in my early twenties in Oxford, when its multifoliate splendor astounded me. It was Dante's *Paradiso* in music, I remember thinking, a great luminous sea of shifting and mounting ecstatic sound. This afternoon, in Ma's house, with our conversation about music and the music of Reality still fresh in my spirit, I heard the Tallis as if for the first time, as if with her ears.

I was sitting in my chair looking at Ma's photograph as I listened. At once, as the music began, the photograph started to emit great waves of Light. The Light possessed my mind and body, and I heard the music not without me but within my Heart.

Her voice: *In my silence all the voices of the world rise in ecstasy. In my silence all the voices of the world are reconciled.*

Each voice in the sublime motet sang in perfectly lucid ecstatic harmony with every other voice, forming endlessly changing transforming masses of illumined ripe sound.

*In the new creation souls will sing together like this.*

I heard spiral after spiral of ascending glorious sound rise calmly, with a passion at once detached and supremely intense, from its bed of Silence, rise, commingle in bliss, and finally culminate in the vast prolonged cry of Light on Light at the end of the work, a cry that does not end but seems to reverberate, like the OM I had heard at Mahabalipuram, throughout the cosmos forever.

Her voice: *I am the light entering matter. I am matter. I am matter spiraling back to myself. I am each creature I carry and transfigure. This is the music of my divine transformation.*

Ten minutes later I was walking up the road that leads to Mr. Reddy's samadhi when I saw Ma and Adilakshmi coming down the other way. I felt suddenly afraid of crossing her, of meeting her eye, afraid of being plunged into another experience as demanding or more so than what had already occurred that afternoon. A voice within said, I cannot stand anymore: I will break. Immediately my saner self began to smile. Why am I still afraid? Won't she know exactly how much I can bear?

Ma came toward me in the gray morning street, and I felt my heart pulse and contract as if she had put her hand into my chest and were squeezing it lightly but firmly. Waves of bliss began to move up and down my body.

We passed. Idiotically I said, "You are coming down from Mr. Reddy; I am going up to him." Ma turned toward me, stopped for a moment, and smiled with an intensity so extreme, it took all my strength to hold it. Everything—the street, the two black cars between which she was standing, her own body and Adilakshmi's—seemed to vanish for that moment; only the smile remained. I bowed my head to her in gratitude. She nodded slightly, turned, and walked casually on.

At once my mind became entirely silent, very wide. I looked at everything around me—the cars, the gardens, the iron fence around the church—as if I had never seen them before and did not know what they were.

Slowly I walked up to Mr. Reddy's grave.

As I walked I heard her voice say:

*As you awaken, all those you love awaken a little with you. All those you love are linked by that love, are on the same spiral, rising.*

My heart filled with joy, for I knew in that moment that no awakening can be personal or selfish. Every awakening spreads its power and light throughout the world.

Three fat old ladies were sweeping the cemetery and chattering. Their ordinary talk was wonderfully comforting and mysterious; I leaned back into it. Love for the women filled my being, for each fold of their cheeks, their old hands, their comfortable cheap clothes. I felt this silent love enter them, warm them secretly. She was allowing me, I saw, to love for these few moments with some small part of her Force. I knew then that the Power of Love was not just a phrase—that if this force could be sustained, all things around it would be altered.

I walked into the landscape of fields and woods beyond the cemetery. I sat down on a bench I often sat on, one that overlooks the whole of Thalheim.

Looking out with a silent mind across the fields and hills and roads, I knew them all as One Thing appearing in different forms and shapes. Each thing, as each voice in the Tallis had been, was almost preternaturally precise; nothing lost its individuality, yet each thing was made of the same substance, was moving and breathing and shining and emerging in and from the same vast, quiet Body. I gazed at the large green field opposite, as if drawn to it by some secret force. The outlines of Her Face appeared in it, in great strokes of white light, as if the rich turf had been parted to reveal what was underneath.

*All this is me. You looking at it are looking at it within me. These eyes you are seeing my face with are my eyes. You are looking at yourself within me with your real eyes.*

The phrases rose and commingled and revealed new identities, new harmonies within me effortlessly, as the voices had in the Tallis. "Mine" and "Hers" became inseparable, the same deep, quiet sound formed by differently shaped lips.

As a small, helpless sign of gratitude I went to a flower shop and bought some pink gladioli for Ma and walked with them a little unsteadily to the house. I could not help wondering if

I would "see" her, if she would "close" the experiences in some way, with a gesture or a glance.

Ma was squatting in front of the house, fixing the kitchen window from the outside. I realized that was exactly what I now had to do—fix my inner window, see that it stayed steady.

*Always you must balance what I give you. Integrate it, bring it into the real.*

I went inside to put the flowers in a vase. I needed a large vase and could not remember ever having seen one large enough for these flowers. I went up to the *darshan* room. There by the throne were two enormous dark red jars I had never seen before. They must have been lying outside somewhere or in the shed. They were in the shapes of spirals.

# NINE

In late September 1987 I returned to Paris to pay bills, see old friends passing through. The Process continued. Each day it became fiercer, so fierce sometimes that my body felt shredded, and I had to lie down for long periods on my bed in my room, waiting for the new strength that always followed.

My first night back Adilakshmi told me in a dream that I still did not know how to surrender. She spoke kindly but with a chilling clarity, saying: "Behind all your gestures there is always still the I; you must learn to ask for nothing." I woke up, feeling desolate, realizing the truth of everything she had said. My room was full of moonlight, and I asked Ma to help me surrender, to give everything. "I know that on my own I cannot give myself; you must empower me." Then I fell asleep.

This time Ma came into the dream. She was dressed in a red sari, and we were walking up a snow-covered slope. She gestured for me to sit down. Then she said, "Well, what did you think of the dream I just gave you when Adilakshmi said . . ."

I was so shocked I woke up. For a moment I was terrified. Then I began to laugh. How many times had I begged her in *darshan* to possess my consciousness, to live in every part of my mind and body?

Two days later a book arrived in the mail that I had ordered months before and forgotten about—Irina Tweedie's *Daughter of Fire*. Tweedie's book is the most moving and accurate account of a spiritual transformation at the hands of a Great Master that I have read. Over the next days in Paris I devoured it. So many strange and marvelous parallels existed between our experiences. I recognized the same signs of Change—the Sound, the days of bliss, the deep, painful longing, the bouts of wild irritation with oneself and everyone else that come under the stress of real transformation, the penetration by the Master of all the levels of awareness.

"It is the task of the Teacher," Tweedie writes, "to set the heart aflame with the unquenchable fire of longing, and it is his duty to keep it burning until it is reduced to ashes. For only a heart that has burned empty is capable of love."

I understand what Adilakshmi had meant in my dream: I was not yet burned empty. I understood, too, why Ma had appeared in the red sari on the slope of snow: She was signaling to me my lucid entry into her Fire. My task now was to walk into it without wavering and burn.

 On the plane back to Frankfurt, four weeks later, a Sufi story Tweedie tells kept coming back to me.

A king had a slave he loved a great deal. He ordered all his slaves and courtiers to come to a courtyard. There he spread a variety of treasures. He said, "Just touch anything, and you can have it." One man touched a priceless Persian carpet, another a throne, and were given them and went away singing. The slave he loved sat and did nothing. Then the king asked him, "What do you want?" Silently the slave came and touched the king on his shoulder.

I had to become that slave, I realized. I had to want not the marvelous new powers she was pouring into my mind and body nor the revelations that satisfied my spirit, nor even the beautiful and intricate drama of "Lover" and "Beloved" I was enacting with her, but her herself, her essence, Union.

In all other states something of the ego remained, as "enjoyer" or "actor," "dancer" or "devotee." Only in Union would the ego also be gone.

"No one ever gets more than what they want," Irina Tweedie's Master had told her. I had to have the courage, I saw, to want everything, to want her.

🕉 I arrived at Thalheim in the middle of an overcast, quiet afternoon and went to find Ma. She was standing in dusty work clothes by the side of the house, with a drill in her hand. Daniel, dramatically thinner and grinning, stood by her.

"While you swan around the world," he joked, "we workers actually *do* something."

I could not take my eyes from Ma's face. There was dust from the drilling in her hair. She returned my gaze unsmilingly, then soberly nodded.

*So far so good. You have seen and understood. And now for the next part.*

I moved into a new room downstairs looking out onto the street. That night I had a dream whose imagery and power were to recur in many forms throughout the next weeks.

The dream began in a large amphitheater, like the Colosseum. There were thousands of people, a lot of noise. In one of the boxes, the Imperial Box, perhaps, I saw a hollow statue with a vast crown on it studded with rubies. Feeling brave, I found a way into the box and started to collect all the rubies and put them into a bag. I looked at the crown when I had finished. It was empty and hollow, as insignificant as a bit of iron railing left at a building site. People started to chase me.

I kept thinking: The rubies are Ma's color; the color of Durga, the Mother; they rightly belong to her.

At that moment I found myself in a large, fragrant summer garden, like the garden of St. John's College in Oxford, which was full of sunlight and flowers. I wandered about it and then lay on the grass, breathing the clear air. I closed my eyes, then opened them. There Ma was, extremely beautiful, her hair streaming out in the wind, in a gold-and-red sari. Behind her, to the left, a small girl was playing in a white dress.

I stood up and handed the jewels that had now become one vast uncut ruby to Ma. She smiled and, without looking at it, handed it to the small girl to play with. Then, smiling, with her arms quietly outstretched, she turned and started to walk toward me. I seemed to be vanishing completely into a burning golden Light. I kept thinking, "I cannot bear this. I will die," but her Force held me there. Fear gave way to calm joy. I heard her voice: *I do not love you for what you do or win for me. I do not love you for your devotion. I love you as you are, unconditionally.*

Daniel and I, a few days later, had our first fight. I came out of the house after a morning of reading and meditation and he said, "Don't you ever do anything useful?"

He had unnerved me, and I shouted at him.

Later he came into my room and apologized.

"Actually I was only making a joke. God knows, I know how useful meditation is."

He sat down on the bed.

"This is a period of strain for both of us. We must be kind to each other."

"In my whole life," I said, "I have never felt so strung out."

"I feel the same way. So much is changing."

Drilling began at the side of the house. We looked at each other.

"My body is changing," he said quietly.

"It is amazing how much thinner you have gotten since I went away."

"It's more than that. My body is changing."

I stared at him. "What do you mean?"

"About two months ago," Daniel said, "I came in the house after work and this Force fell onto my body. It was almost as if a tiger had sprung out of the stairs and leapt on me. I was frightened. I went and lay down. Fire played up and down my body, intensely. Then afterward I felt very soft, relaxed. This went on happening again and again. What is going on? I kept asking her inwardly. Slowly I realized: my body is being transformed. The Light is entering my body to *change* it. I realized also that the reason it was causing me pain was that I was in bad condition. I've allowed myself to get fat these last years. I had to lose weight, to allow the Force room."

He paused.

"I've been with her eight years, but in these last weeks I feel I have at last understood something. This Force she is bringing down is going to change everything."

We sat in silence listening to the traffic.

"We are going through parallel transformations," Daniel said. "Don't you dare go faster than me."

The drilling at the side of the house got louder and then stopped.

"I used to imagine myself," I said, "sitting cross-legged, undisturbed, in a monastery in Ladakh. But the change I had been praying for is happening to the sound of drilling in a German village."

Daniel stood silently.

"What are you waiting for?" I asked him.

The drilling began again.

"That," he said, grinning.

Later that afternoon I went for a walk in the rain. As I walked I felt my body become peaceful. The gray of the landscape now seemed sweet and gentle, like old Chinese silk. I entered lovingly into the gray mist, the mud, the rain pouring down. The cold wind blowing into my face, which half an hour ago would have made me flinch and grit my teeth, became an exotic luxury, a sensation to be savored.

Then briefly I saw it. All the trees and fields were giving off white light, the light I had seen at *darshan*, that streamed from her photograph.

I was beginning to see reality consciously as divine, as an emanation of light.

The next night, in Daniel's room, began a series of increasingly fierce and exultant experiences with the Divine Light. Daniel had put a new photograph of Ma above his bed, one in which she is unsmiling, molten, furious, dressed in a purple sari and with a long rope of pearls that hangs down the sari like the rope of skulls on medieval Bengali paintings of Kali. I had never seen it before, and it shook me.

While Daniel read the paper I meditated on his bed in front of this image. Very quickly Ma's face began to stream with burning golden light. The Face started to swim rapidly in fire toward me, to vanish into me and reappear, its savage beauty always more and more powerful. The whole room that I know so well—in the bachelor disorder Daniel always keeps it— began to vanish into waves of boiling golden Light. The Face withdrew its Power. Daniel turned on the news, and I watched the day's events with an exaggerated attention, as if finding my way slowly back to reality.

In the two weeks that followed, the Light returned, again and again, sometimes ten or twelve times daily.

I would be warned by Her sound suddenly humming in the air around me. Then, from one of her photographs, the Light would stream, in a diamond-white torrent, compelling me to sit or lie down wherever I was. I had to give myself over to it completely. There was no choice.

My first instinct was often terror, but with the Light came Knowledge. The Divine Light was now operating on me to teach me directly. I called the Light my Lion. It could, at any moment, unsheathe its radiance and spring.

The most sacred moment had arrived in my journey. Aurobindo speaks of the time when the Divine shows that It has accepted the sacrifice of the devotee and takes up his or her spiritual discipline itself, when the Light, instead of being hidden or occasionally manifest, becomes increasingly present, constant, and visible to the naked physical eye. All excuses for ignorance, all fantasies of inadequacy or abandonment were now to be stripped from me.

Repeatedly in those weeks I remembered something I had seen in my childhood in India—a tree in our garden in Hyderabad being struck by lightning again and again and turning, as if in rapture, in the direction of the lightning, flinging up every branch and leaf toward the Fire that was destroying it. I was that tree now, turning my whole self to the Fire that was eating me alive. I knew that my being would be irreversibly turned toward That now, as the tree had been; that certainty and the rapture it brought helped me to bear the suffering that came, helped me to enter it again and again without fear. Terror turned into thirst for the Glory of the Presence, however annihilating; thirst and a gratitude as visceral and immense as the Fire itself.

A book arrived from a friend in England halfway through this Burning, which described to me exactly its operation: St. John of the Cross's *Living Flame of Love*.

St. John compares the soul to a log of wood that has to be first penetrated by the fire and then consumed in it. The log is initially always dank and dirty and has first to be prepared by the fire before the Fire can enter it.

Passages from the book instructed me how to bear the sometimes terrifying desolation the Fire brought with it, the sense of helpless unworthiness, exhaustion, self-disgust.

"In this preparatory state of purgation the flame is not bright to it (the Soul) but dark. Neither is it sweet to it, but grievous; for though at times it kindles within it the heat of love, this is accompanied by torment and affliction. And it is not delectable to it, but arid; it brings with it neither refreshment nor peace, but consumes and accuses it; neither is it glorious to it but rather makes it miserable and bitter by means of the spiritual light of self-knowledge that it sheds upon it."

The Fire is a mirror in which all the cruelties and subtle madness of the ego are seen, with no possibility of evasion or consolation. I lived again through my long betrayal of Her, all the ways I still looked to use or evade her, the grief of my sexual and creative life, the sullen hypocrisies I had cherished in myself.

Throughout this agony I could never forget everything I knew of Her Mercy. I knew a power as loving as hers would never wound except to heal; would never strip me unless to clothe me in richness and splendor; would never make me cry out again and again in grief unless the death this brought was to prepare an infinitely wider life.

The Fire of love strips the log it has prepared and then enters it. The soul that has nearly died of grief and shame now nearly dies of the love it feels piercing and opening its inmost secret center. It knows at this moment, with a self-evident certainty, that it is entering into union with its source, the Fire of Eternal Love and Knowledge.

"For inasmuch as this flame is a flame of the Divine Life, it wounds the soul with the tenderness of the life of God; and so deeply . . . does it wound it and fill it with tenderness that it causes it to melt in love, so that there may be fulfilled in it that which came to pass in the Bride in the Song of Songs; she conceived such great tenderness that she melted away."

During this extraordinary, prolonged rapture Ma also faced me again with the worst trait in my character—my pride.

I longed at that time to be able to communicate what I was coming to know of Ma's glory, but I was made to understand inwardly that I must keep silent from now on in the Process, for to communicate anything to anyone except Ma and Adilakshmi would risk scorn or bewilderment or a jealousy that could be dangerous.

Instead of reassuring me as it was meant to, this enforced reticence made me boil with rage. Because I was becoming aware so acutely of my own secret cowardice and treachery, I also became aware of the cowardice, depression, evasion, laziness in everyone around me. Since I was finding part of my own nature intolerable in this new intimacy with the Light, I found everyone else intolerable also. I was forced to realize that I had marred nearly every human relationship I had had by an impatience with imperfection, a rage against human dullness and stupidity; I was forced to realize that this rage itself was neurotic, an evasion of the harder work of love, and of my own stupidity, which took more secret forms. My longing to enthuse the others with the beauty of what I was being shown could mask a secret desire to impress, or even to humiliate them by the difference between the passion of my experience with Her and theirs; could veil a desire for spiritual power that was as dangerous, or more so, than their ordinary dullness; could hide a desire on my part to revenge myself for the months of boredom or irritation they had caused me, which was not their fault, after all, and as much a result of the imbalance of my temperament as theirs.

Yet each time I felt the difficulty of change was too great, the Light would descend and sweep me to where I could watch the death of the old self with detachment and sometimes even hilarity.

ॐ Halfway through this period, Mother's younger brother Raju arrived from India to live with her and Adilakshmi. Ma gave me the task of teaching him English.

Raju reminded me of the lanky, huge-eyed Indian boys I had played with as a child, and I grew to love him. Taking him on walks in the autumn sunlight and teaching him *cow* and *sheep* and *wall* and *stream* made me reexperience the wonder of language. My hours with him focused and balanced days that were otherwise spent out of time.

I wrote: "In having me teach Raju, Ma is showing me what she is doing—teaching me a language with rules, declensions, marvelous precisions. She is showing me it is as normal an activity as walking with Raju in the fields pointing out to him flowers and animals he may not have seen before, explaining what they are, and bearing with him as he mispronounces their names until he gets them right."

These hours with Raju also gave me the chance to see Ma herself at a time when I needed to. It was inexpressibly comforting to see her come in from gardening, to drink tea with her silently after a lesson with Raju, or to talk about the weather or the designs for the new house she was planning to construct.

Every time I stumbled upstairs to see her taking off her boots or adjusting the door of a cupboard, her lips puckered fiercely, I was compelled to see that what I was undergoing was both miraculous and natural.

"Fear is going," I said to her one day, saying something serious for the first time in days.

"It will go," she said, not looking up from her book.

"I am going sane," I said.

She laughed, going on reading.

"May I come and talk to you tomorrow at eight o'clock?"

"Why not?"

On the next evening Adilakshmi met me at the door. Ma was sitting with her back to us, in a green-and-red sari. I walked around her to the sofa and sat facing her.

I prayed to her inwardly to make me clear.

Then I asked her: "Is it true that anyone who gives him- or herself to you will have similar experiences to the ones I have had, in terms of their own temperaments and in their own rhythm?"

"Yes. Many things will be the same. Emphasis will sometimes be different."

"My temperament is passionate and dramatic, so you have taught me in my own terms. Another calmer temperament you would teach in another way."

"Yes, yes,"—Ma was laughing—"you are fiery."

I looked down at her hands folded in stillness in her lap.

"You are never tired of repeating things with me, even when I fail." My voice trembled.

"Failing is not important. Everyone will fail for some time. Everyone will make mistakes. But you must not be discouraged. You must never think 'I cannot do this.' You must know it is not you doing the work; it is the Mother. You must have faith in Her."

She opened her hand. "You must work like this."

I looked at her fingers. They were completely without tension.

"To work like that," I said, "demands total trust."

Ma nodded.

Tears came to my eyes. "I have never felt forced by you. I have felt amazed, astonished, afraid—but never forced."

"The Divine never forces. The ego forces. The Divine is patient."

"The Divine does not force the human because it knows the human really is Itself. The Divine does not do violence to Itself."

Then I said. "When this Process is complete, will I, as your Child, be the Master, under you, of my own evolution?"

"Yes, I am lighting a flame," she said, looking directly into my eyes. "Once the flame is lit, nothing can put it out."

I could ask no more questions. "May I come again tomorrow?" I said eventually.

"You can come whenever you want."

ॐ That night I dreamed I went to an empty hall where Ma was standing at the end with two bowls of dark, bloody liquid before her.

I realized looking at the bowls that they contained all the evil and grief of the world, everything in humankind that hated the Divine and resisted the Light.

Calmly, looking at me, she raised them both to her lips and drank. I was terrified. Her body changed color, withered, seemed to bend over and crackle in the horror of what she was allowing to be done to her. I tried to move toward her, but my feet felt nailed to the ground.

"Ma," I cried. "Ma," and closed my eyes.

When I opened them, she was standing, as calmly as before, as beautiful. She pointed to the two bowls that still stood before her.

In each of them was a liquid I had never seen before, gold, luminous.

"Drink yourself," she said, "and then give this wine to everyone else. It will never run out now."

I bent over the shining gold liquid and saw reflected in its mirror her face, with mine inside it. As I gazed my face vanished, and faces of every nationality, color, and type took its place. Her face remained.

"What you drink, all will drink. I have prepared this wine of the Mother for the world."


I woke filled with awe and compassion for Ma, for the suffering the dream had revealed to me, for the price she paid at every moment to be here. I went over in my mind all the moments I had glimpsed this depth of sacrifice in her—Adilakshmi saying, "Ma is always alone"; Mr. Reddy saying, "You cannot imagine what she has been through in a body. I saw it"; Daniel saying, "Without her being here this would be impossible. Imagine what she gives up."

I determined that night to ask her about her suffering. I knew what I would be asking was the most intimate question of all, but I had to ask it. I had to know, so my love for her could be complete.

Ma welcomed me that evening in a red sari.

She sat on the sofa and I sat next to her.

For a long moment I could say nothing. Then I began, "I wanted to ask you about your suffering, about what and why you suffer. The words sound ridiculous when I say them. Forgive me."

She smiled. "There is nothing to forgive. You want to understand."

"Yes," I said. "I want to understand so I can love more."

We sat for a long time in tender silence.

"You, as an avatar, chose to do the work of the Transformation knowing it would be terrible and hard."

"Yes."

"Knowing every evil force would be pitted against you, every resistance, every madness in the mind of humankind."

"Yes," she said very softly, "all this I knew."

"You knew, too, that you, in your body, your human body, would have to undergo all the suffering necessary for the Light to be brought down."

"Yes."

"I understand now that to be able to bear pain is necessary for the Transformation."

"There will be pain. You must bear it."

"But the pain you bear must be greater than my human pain because of the Divine Presence in you."

Very quietly Ma said, looking down at her hands, "For

physical pain you can get medicine. For Divine Pain what medicine is there?"

I had never heard her complain of anything. The enormity of what she was saying tore open my heart.

"Oh, my God," I cried. We were silent a long time.

Ma continued to look down at her hands.

"I have not wanted to imagine your suffering sometimes," I finally said, "because I did not want to face your love. Sometimes your disciples say, 'Ma is divine; she does not suffer; she is beyond suffering,' but this is an evasion of you, of what you are, and is cowardice. They—we—neither want to face your love nor what we will have to bear to change."

"You must bear," Ma said quietly.

"Your suffering is born out of love and is always transformed, isn't it, into the bliss of love?"

"Yes."

"By offering it, you transform suffering into ananda?"

"There is no offering. Suffering comes from the Supreme; both Light and Pain come from there. I cannot offer it. The avatar has a dharma, a duty, like everyone else. You are a teacher; you must bear the pain of being a teacher. An avatar must bear the pain of being an avatar. This is my part in the Play. I must bear whatever comes. I must accept everything."

"And by seeing how you bear your pain for your work, I will learn how to bear the pain my work must bring. I will learn how always to offer it to you."

"Yes," she said gently, "you have the chance to offer your pain to me."

She paused and added, almost inaudibly, "But I cannot offer my pain to anybody."

In all the years of our love it was in that moment that I felt most close to her. I wanted to reach out and kiss her hands, but I knew such a gesture was absurd. She had accepted so completely her pain, and with a clarity beyond the reach of pity. She was alone in her majesty and always would be.

For a long time there was nothing to say.

Then Ma said: "You, too, must learn to suffer what is necessary with joy and give everything I give you away. The richest inside give the most; this is the Divine Way."

She smiled and raised the second finger of her right hand and waved it gently at me. "No escape, Andrew, no escape."

She stood up. The conversation was over. I stopped in the doorway to look at her one last time. She turned and gazed at me.

"You must never forget," she said, "one moment of these hours you have spent with me."

"Fill every corner of my mind and being with you."

She nodded.

"I am asking you to kill the old mind and to fill it with nothing but you!"

She nodded once more, lowered her eyes, and I left the room.

A few hours later, unable to sleep, I walked up into the woods. Great arcs of Divine Light shone above the hills. The path in front of me shimmered and vibrated, a long river of light.

As if by an order, I turned my head toward a great hollow in the hills in which I had often sat. A streaming white comet of Light fell into it.

*This is my light. It is hitting the whole world, entering wherever it can.*

I knelt in the snow.

*Go on kneeling. Keep looking in front of you.*

Slowly, with marvelous wit and delicacy, different-colored lights began to sweep the great expanse of snow before me— a deep, soft red, a pink, a white, a green softer and more fragrant than the first birch leaves.

*The Mother is playing with her child. Our games now will be games of light.*

Turbulent days followed. I was astonished. I had imagined that, after the glory of my two conversations with Ma, the ascent would be, if not easy, at least much smoother than before. This was an illusion of my ego; I had to be purified again and again.

One afternoon I went out walking, unable to endure my smell or presence any longer. It was dark and gray, and immediately all my suppressed loathing of a certain side of Germany came to a boil in my mind. I cursed the rain, the gloom of the cities, the depression and despair etched on almost every face. I cursed X's hypochondria, U's dullness, the terrible gloomy stupidity that rose like marsh gas from the pointless half conversations in the kitchen and elsewhere. I wanted to be anywhere, anywhere on earth but here with these people, with this sense of pervasive sickness and evasion around me. I walked up into the gloom of a dark avenue of trees, and my rage deepened into a panic more frightening than any I had ever experienced.

Images rose in my mind—images of the concentration camps, which I had been repressing throughout my stay in Germany. I was living panic, the panic of those being led to their deaths in gas chambers under similar dark skies in the rain. I realized how much of my rage at the German disciples had been my fear of the Nazi past shadowing them; my rage at their depression had been a rage at its source—a guilt at the Holocaust so deep, it could not be admitted. And to confront that anger I had to go through my own final fear of what had happened.

With that insight the experience turned. I understood how my rage was itself bestial, how it was projecting the horror onto the trees, into the clouds of the sky that seemed to be pressing closer. The disgust of the afternoon was my own inner horror projected outward. Fear and hatred had created the gas chambers; my fear and hatred were creating this gas chamber in which I was suffocating. I experienced directly the power of the mind to fashion reality. Each wave of rage was exactly accompanied by a wave of darkness thrown at me from the trees or the lurching path in front of me.

My madness and the German madness and the madness of the West were not separate; they were part of the same mad mind that was destroying the ozone layer, burning the forests of the Amazon, polluting every landscape, every sea, every child's mind, in every culture.

If I fought against this mind with fury and scorn, I would be expressing its darkness from another angle; I would be the victim of my own terror. Ma was making me face the killer that still remained in myself, that wanted to kill the Child to which she was trying to give birth.

I had to end, forever, the reign of this killer in myself, if the Child was to be born. Only then would the trees stop swaying sickeningly and the strength to endure the inevitable destruction of this dying and scared civilization be given. For that strength to be there, every movement of hatred has to end, every movement of panic or fear has to vanish.

The experience ceased. The afternoon became an ordinary winter afternoon: my affection for X and U returned; the trees regained their calm truth. I felt the wet earth under my feet and heard the song of birds drifting across the fields.

That evening at *darshan* I prayed, "Kill the killer; I am ready." At last I meant it.

 That night I had a dream, at once hilarious and terrifying, signaling the end of one kind of creative life.

It opened with me sitting with a famous Russian poet friend

who loathes mysticism, drinks too much, and worships at the shrine of irony. He was leering at me across an ill-lit table and egging me on to drink more and more brandy. Weakly, feeling absurd, I was doing so. He was raving against God—brilliantly and humorously—and I could not help laughing. I got drunker. At one moment he leaned over the table to me and said with scorn, "And who is your Master?"

I realized at once that I was going to have to tell the truth or betray everything I had been living. And yet to tell the truth was to have all the acerbic wit I had been laughing at unleashed against me.

"I don't have a Master," I said, feeling sick.

But he took hold of the scruff of my jacket. "Who is your Master?" he repeated.

I remembered Ma's face, so beautiful and lonely, when she had said, "For Divine Pain what medicine is there?"

"My Master," I said quietly, "is Mother Meera."

At that moment the door of the vast, empty room in which we were talking blew open, shattering the lamp on the table. And in the moonlight of the door I saw a man completely dressed in black on a horse with my body draped across it.

I was terrified. But then a voice said: *Look at the body.* It was made of papier-mâché, with red paint stains on it, and the horse itself, which had at first seemed powerful, a horse out of hell, was a machine made of dark-green plasticine.

I awoke, drenched in sweat.

But I am not dead. I laughed. I am more alive than I have ever been.


Late that same afternoon I was sitting in one of the wooden watchtowers in the woods.

Three young deer came out of the shadows and walked

calmly to lie down in drifts of golden leaves fifty yards from the tower. They remained there, silent, unmoving, a long time in a pool of brimming dusk light that seemed both to ring and protect them as well as to emanate from their own peace.

*Be like them*, I heard her say. *Move with dignity into your own splendor.*

# TEN

The next afternoon I went at three o'clock to teach Raju English. He had done no work but improvised shrewdly. Ma sat listening in the chair opposite, reading another English book and mouthing the words to herself. Sometimes she would lean over, smile, and translate what I was trying to say to Raju into telugu. Sometimes she would go into quiet peals of laughter. She was wearing one of the saris Adilakshmi had painted—with large red blossoms—and a baggy brown sweater. Her hair was down.

When the lesson was over, I was about to go, but Ma asked me to have some tea.

I looked over to her. "If I stay, you know I will ask you questions. I can't help myself, Ma."

She became serious. The beautiful relaxed girl she had been a moment before changed into an older woman with quiet, deep eyes.

The room grew still.

"I wanted to ask you how your grace works."

"How it works?" Ma was amused.

Ma was looking at me concentratedly.

"There is a way, isn't there," I said, "in which your grace works automatically? This Force you have brought down onto the earth is there to be called on by all those who love you."

"Yes," Ma said strongly. "This is so. The Grace works automatically when the aspiration is sincere. It is not necessary for me always to know. Too much knowledge can bring complications, no?"

"If you knew consciously at every moment everything that was being done by your Force and in its name, it would create confusion."

"Yes," she said. "But I can know what I want when I want and when I need."

"But there are still things you have to learn on *this* level, aren't there? How to speak English, how to put in a plug, how to make a chapati."

"A chapati I know how to make,"—Ma laughed—"and English I am learning more and more."

"What I meant was this, Ma: I could teach you how to type badly with two fingers. So there is a very unequal but real exchange. It's part of your Play, isn't it, to allow us to help you?"

"Yes." Ma was smiling.

"So by helping you, aren't we really only giving you what has always been yours? You are allowing us to give to you for our sake."

Her smile widened. "Yes. So you can learn the joy of giving."

"But the more we see that the giving is not ours, the more we do not own our giving, the freer we are?"

"Yes."

There was silence.

She read my thoughts and said, "Neither you nor I will die. The actors in a play do not die. They change clothes, no? They say and do what the Writer tells them to, no?"

The clouds of the early afternoon had parted. A late sunlight filled the room.

Ma handed me a red-and-gold sweet. I noted the color and smiled. I ate the sweet in silence, then got up to go.

"Thank you," Ma said. "You are explaining things. You are making things clear."

I was overwhelmed.

"Whatever clarity I may have, Ma, comes from your Light."

"This is true," she said ruefully, as if sad to admit it. "But you are learning to reflect it; that is a great thing."

I was standing in the doorway, swaying a little.

"Ma," I said, gazing into her eyes, "the world is in pain. Only your Force can save it. Will you save it?"

Ma turned to me, and the transformation in her face and body was extraordinary. She was exultant, fiery with Light that burned along her hair and shoulders.

"I will save it," she said.


That night I had the most disturbing of all the dreams I received in her house. S, a woman I had loved and lived with, who had drunk too much out of misery and was obsessed to the point of psychosis by the apocalypse, came into my room in the dream and sat, swaying, on the end of my bed. Her wit and savagery had terrified me during our relationship, and again that terror returned.

"I have come," she said, "to flay you alive. Fools deserve to be flayed."

And she began a tirade against everything I was learning.

"You deserve to die," she screamed. "We are all going to die. Our eyeballs are all going to run like dirty water down our faces. We are evil rats that deserve to be exterminated."

I awoke sweating and got out of my bed. Kneeling to Ma, I prayed to her to take away my pain.

*As you get closer to me, doubts try and claim you. Watch these doubts. Use their violent energy against them.*

How can there be any room for doubt in my mind, I asked her, when I have seen so much?

*Doubt doubt with S's fury and you will be free of doubt and her. Turn the dogs of doubt on doubt. Take the sword of doubt from the ego's hand and cut down the ego with it.*

I sat up in bed, rehearsing all that S had said. With chilling exactitude I now saw which parts of me had conspired with the version of Reality S had always offered me, and I offered them up for transformation.

Peace came slowly, and with it the first pale streams of dawn.

That afternoon Ma again came in after Raju's English lesson, and we had tea. I told her of the night I had been through.

"Doubt is useful," Ma said after I had finished. "It keeps you honest. Sometimes people say how much they love me and love God, but I know what is in their hearts. It is better when someone says "I love you" knowing all the doubt still within them. Then it means something. Then love can grow."

She smiled tenderly. "I know how hard it is for the human being now to believe."

"Doubt always tries to destroy after a great leap forward has been made—my old self tries to kill what I see."

"Your old self comes up again *to be killed*," she said, smiling broadly. "It knows it is lying."

She gave me some tea.

I started to laugh.

"Why are you laughing?"

"I am laughing at the perfection of your work. How you turn terror into blessing, doubt into progress."

"If doubt did not come, faith would be very . . ."—she

searched for the word and then pointed to the tea—"Faith would be like this tea—not hot at all."

"Lukewarm."

She repeated the word. " 'Lukewarm.' Little can be done with the 'lukewarm.' "

"All doubts now," I said, "are painful."

"End the pain," Ma said, "by going deeper into the Light."

Adilakshmi opened the window to the late afternoon, and the room filled with cool wind.

"I have come to see," I began, "that there are three stages in our love, yours and mine. First, I meet you and feel something of your beauty. Second, this love for you and your much greater and more powerful love for me mingle and lead me into your being and so into my own. Next, I discover that you and I are not separate; that we are One." My voice sounded ridiculous in its precision. I added, with embarrassment, "This third stage is the one you are leading me into, isn't it?"

"Yes." She smiled. "And there is a fourth stage."

"And what is that?"

*Watch my hands.*

I watched her hands. They joined completely, tightly, all the fingers interlocking. Then they parted and opened again, still joined at the wrist.

For a moment I simply stared. Then I understood. "The journey toward you begins in duality," I said, "deepens into Unity, and then opens again into duality, this time lit with a knowledge of Unity." My hands moved toward each other, closed together, and then opened again like two flowers, joined at the wrist.

She smiled. "It is like that."

"Only for me," I said. "For you the last position has always been true. For you I was always joined to you, inseparable from you."

Ma nodded.

The conversation was over.

I turned in the door. "And now, Ma, I ask you for the Silence behind all words, the Light behind all appearances."

I had not intended to ask for these things so solemnly.

Ma turned around to face me. I realized she was at exactly the same distance as she had been in my dream when she had given the ruby to the child and begun to walk toward me.

"Yes," she said, "ask for everything. There will be more and more."

I could say nothing. I turned and left.

My room downstairs, when I returned to it, was full of the Mother's gold Light. As soon as I walked in I heard Ma's voice: *Look at the dot between my eyes.*

Turning to the photograph of Ma on the wall, I gazed at the large red dot on her forehead between her eyes. I had never concentrated on that spot before.

Ma's eyes became two whirlpools of fire, and the large red circle started to vibrate and burn. Her Force seized me and began to pour itself into me. I felt as if the lid of my head and my entire face had been peeled off and molten radiance was being poured directly into my mind and body.

I was aware of cars passing, but as if at a distance. Only I and the large red circle existed. The universe had dissolved. The circle started to rotate, emitting a steady fire. Then a large parting occurred between the eyebrows, and the circle became the blazing red pupil of a third eye, an eye like a boiling sun.

*This is the Shakti. This is the central force of the cosmos. From this force all things are born.*

The words repeated in my spirit again and again with the Force of a mantra given directly by the Divine.

I gasped and laughed. I had asked Ma for the Silence and Unity behind all words and appearances.

*I am showing you what you wanted to see.*

The image of her throwing me the red balloon returned but now with extreme meaning.

*I am throwing you the red sun.*

*This is your essential nature.*

Ma's voice was clear and majestic in my mind, a voice like a trumpet, not human at all.

The sun-eye grew until it blazed across Ma's entire forehead, filling the room with a red-gold soft light.

*Gaze with all your strength into the eye.*

I summoned up my strength and gazed. The Eye changed and became a violent yet tender red, the red of Durga, the red of the sari Ma wears when I worship her as Durga.

*This is my eye. This is my heart. My heart is an eye. My eye is the force of the universe.*

*Eye and heart and force are one power.*

*This power is birthing the new creation.*

The walls around the Eye became like melting butter, so soft I thought they would dissolve and cover me in their gold.

I heard the sound of the Sea, which I often hear in meditation, a sound like the sea at Mahabalipuram, but now enormously amplified, like the soft, distant roar of a thousand oceans. Through it all the ordinary sounds penetrated—the sounds of children playing, Daniel walking about outside, a song on a car radio.

*This is the sound of the Light as it creates the new world.*

Four hours of splendor passed. Toward the end I heard Ma's voice.

*Go to the book you have on Anandamayi Ma and open it.*

I opened the book at the words *The Divine Mother is usually represented with a third eye between the two eyebrows, indicating divine wisdom.*

The next day was Friday the thirteenth of November.

At five minutes to three I was putting on my shoes in the corridor to go out and mail a letter when I looked up to find Ma. She was dressed in her blue overalls for work. She smiled, bent down in front of me, and fixed the door of the shoe cupboard. She rattled it strongly a few times and then slid it into place.

"Ma," I said, "do you remember when you threw me the red balloon upstairs?"

"Yes," she said, testing the sliding door again.

"Yesterday for the first time I saw your Eye, the Eye of the Goddess."

I was smiling at the happy absurdity of having this conversation in the passageway, with the whine of a drill coming from outside.

Ma nodded.

"I saw the sun of red fire in it. I saw the red fire-circle of the eternal Shakti."

Ma became grave, withdrawn.

We were standing close together. I was two steps lower than she, so we were at the same height.

"When you threw me the balloon, you were throwing me the Shakti, weren't you? You were throwing me the Eye. You were throwing me your essence and my own?"

Ma nodded.

"And now I am beginning to throw back the balloon to you, beginning to play also the Great Game."

Ma laughed suddenly. "Yes, your Eye sees my Eye."

"I cannot see something that I am not also."

"No."

"Your Grace has opened my eye so I can see your Glory."

She averted her eyes.

"In meditation just now," I said, "I saw a circle of light in front of the place in the middle of my forehead where the eye is. This is the open Eye, isn't it? And, when I opened my eyes, the circle was still there in front of me."

"Your Eye is open now, awake. It will never close."

She was smiling.

"This is the beginning of the end of the journey, isn't it? I mean, the end of the first journey, the journey to unity with you."

Ma nodded and bent down to fasten one of her shoes.

"I have understood so many things today," I said. "I have understood that I will soon be able to write because at last I have seen who you are."

Ma laughed. "Yes."

"I had to stop believing I could write my book at all, so you could begin to write it in me, write it with every vision, every experience."

"Yes. Now, soon, you will begin. It will come quietly."

"In your rhythm."

She laughed again. "Yes."

Stepping toward me softly, she stood gazing into my eyes.

"You are my sweet child," she said, "you are my sweet child always."

Bliss filled my body, and I stumbled against Daniel's big muddy khaki shoes.

Ma, bowing her head, went down to the kitchen.

That night at *darshan* I put my head in her hands and said, "Let this journey be over soon."

For the rest of the *darshan* I saw a great diamond of Light turning around her at immense speed, so brilliant at times I feared I would be blinded.

*Keep staring into it*, I heard her voice say. *Your eyes will get used to it.*

At the end of *darshan* the great turning diamond became a soft rose color.

*This is dawn*, I heard her voice say, *dawn on the mountain, the dawn of the future.*

An English friend, F, a writer, had come to see Mother Meera. I took him back to his hotel. "Who do you think she is?" he asked me.

I told him.

"You are seriously sitting there and telling me . . ." His voice trailed off.

"I am saying what I know. What did you feel tonight?"

"I felt she was serious," he said. Then he laughed. "She'd have to be serious. Either she'd be bored to death or getting very rich indeed if she weren't. And I assume she's neither."

F leaned forward. "Andrew, keep what you think you know to yourself. Don't open yourself to slaughter."

I smiled and changed the subject. Later, as I was walking back, a wild storm began. I had to walk bent double against the rain. The terror of the dream with S returned. F's words, "Don't open yourself to slaughter," circled in my brain menacingly. All my still-remaining inability to believe, even after all I had been shown, and on that day, attacked me with the same rage as the rain beating against me.

Oh, God, I kept saying, not now, not on this day.

*Of course it must come on this day. How else will you fight free of it?*

I felt nauseated with fear.

I am not worthy, Ma. I cannot hold the splendor of what you have given.

*Choose me now finally and you will grow to be free of all your fears.*

I felt more alone standing there with the freezing black

rain beating against me than at any other moment of my life.

Kneeling in the mud and rain I prayed to her. "Only your strength in me will make me strong enough to say what must be said."

*You cannot go back.*

*There is nowhere to go back to.*

*You know now who I am.*

Then her laugh and: *Do not be afraid of the dark powers.*

*They can do nothing against me.*

*The word "Victory" has already been written by the Light.*

For all the clarity of her voice within me, I felt far from light and victory, kneeling there in the biting rain, tired and ill.

A vast brutal wall of rain and mist obscured Thalheim and the fields around it, vast and brutal as the ignorance of the world, of matter, of all those things within me and without that resisted revelation and Light, that had resisted them since the beginning of history.

*You must choose me now.*

*Only if you choose me completely*

*will you be strong enough to do what you must do.*

I got up shakily from the mud. "I choose you," I said. "Make me strong."

*Go on choosing me every moment.*

*Then no powers anywhere*

*can harm a hair of your head.*

# ELEVEN

Two days later Daniel and I were sitting, after a long night walk, in his room. I had been telling him of my experience of the Fire.

"What has been going on with you? With the Force in your body?"

"I told you my body is changing," Daniel began. "The Force enters the body with a sort of *whooshing* sound. I can't describe it in any other way." He made a few *shoosh*ing noises. "It enters, then it spreads around the body. I told this to Ma and she said, very casually as usual, 'Yes. It is like injections, isn't it?' I have been terrified. But I've learned how to live with fear. Satprem wrote in his great books about the transformation of the body that the body is the weakest, most endangered place. It is. Every cell has been idiotically saying 'I am going to die' for millions of years, so a force that enters the body trying to change all that is bound to arouse the most terrible resistance. It does. But I really want this change, Andrew.

"The attacks last about twenty minutes. About half an hour later I usually feel wonderful, better than ever before in my life. Sometimes I feel like sobbing with relief. Relief is too small a word. Ecstasy is more like it. The body is in ecstasy in every cell. As if every cell is drinking in light. I realize I have never been in my body. I've used it, played sports with it, bashed it about in judo and sex, taken it on long walks, but never inhabited it. This new body isn't otherwordly at all. It is directly, completely here, alive, vibrant, being played by the Force like a kind of guitar."

His left hand moved for a moment over invisible frets.

"But the amazing thing is," he continued, "that the Light itself gives you the necessary information to negotiate these changes."

"Yes," I said. "Ma is making us engineers of our own transformation, experts on ourselves, partners of the Divine."

Daniel started to smile.

"Some partners. Look at us. We're having what the books describe as the 'Great Experiences.' We should be blissed out, in saffron robes, chanting Sanskrit. In fact, we are walking about like two rabbits who have been hit on the back of the neck. But it's better, more human, this way. I said to Ma a few days ago for the first time how much I loved her and how I was at last starting to understand something of her power."

"What did she say?"

"You know Ma. Very downbeat always. 'Yes, yes,' she said, looking out of the window, smiling. Then she said, 'Don't tell the others; they'll think you're mad.' I knew she didn't mean you. You are going through your fire; I am going through mine. She is winding our transformations around each other so we can help and support each other. You want to know the other thing I have learned for good?"

He put his hand on my shoulder.

"Neither you nor I are special: neither of us are 'yogis'; we've both made endless mistakes and been stupid and ordinary. And yet because of her this astounding thing is happening to us. This means that anyone with goodwill and sincerity (let's give ourselves those, shall we), anyone at all, can have this change now."

The next evening, after *darshan*, Adilakshmi called me to her, smiling.

"I have some good news for you," she said quietly. "Someone wants you to teach her English."

"I'd be delighted to teach you English," I said, "but your English is already so good."

"No . . ." Adilakshmi laughed and pointed upward.

She turned and walked, smiling, upstairs.

Then she stopped.

"The first lesson is in twenty minutes."

I went into my room to compose myself. This was the last thing I had expected from Ma, especially at this time in my journey with her when I was becoming continually conscious of her majesty. How could I teach her anything twenty minutes after I had seen the Divine Light burning around her?

*I am teaching you my language. Won't you teach me yours?*

At that I started to laugh.

Ma had found again the perfect way of healing me—by taking me closer still into her intimacy. I could hide from her power or at least run from it, but her love, this endlessly inventive and wise love of hers, would always find me.

Adilakshmi opened the door. Ma was sitting on the sofa behind her, with the English book we would use already open on her lap. She had changed clothes from *darshan* and now wore one of Adilakshmi's hand-painted saris—silver with purple roses.

I had never seen her more beautiful or peaceful. Ma turned

and smiled up at me. Everything in the room seemed softer than before—the light on the chairs, the feel of the sofa, her smile.

The hour that followed was the happiest I had ever spent with her. We practiced the great yogic words together—*serenity, ecstasy, contentment*—repeating them to each other on the sofa. Ma's voice is so naturally gentle, it is difficult for her to pronounce the hard syllables in English words, so we practiced *throat, bark, grip*. She often uses the word *bear*, so I taught her to say *endure*. She learns, as she does everything, simply, without any pretense to knowledge she may not have and with a great quiet concentration.

Ma was teaching me to learn as she did—unhurriedly, relaxedly, unafraid of making mistakes, with humor. Often she would make small mistakes in pronunciation and would look across at me and smile as if to say "See, it is not so serious to make mistakes as you imagine, not so terrible."

I realized also that she was allowing me to love her in another way, to love her as Mr. Reddy had loved her, as a marvelous child. I would find myself almost sternly asking her to repeat a word or a phrase, or to follow the movement of my mouth, and she would do it painstakingly. Only afterward would I realize to *whom* I had been talking with such authority, and I would look across at her and see her eyes full of amusement. I had loved her as my Master, my Friend, my Beloved. I had seen her as the Divine Mother. Now she was letting me see her as a child. This awoke an inexpressible tenderness in me, a tenderness, which, when I remembered it, soothed my panic and fear.

ॐ On the next day I had just finished my lesson with Raju when Ma came in and stood by the window, looking out. We stood a moment silently.

The silence parted and I found myself saying: "The key to

transformation is acceptance, isn't it? And this acceptance brings the awareness that everything you send—grief, disaster, suffering of all kinds—is for our good."

Ma nodded.

"Mr. Reddy came into your being because he always saw your face of love behind and through everything that happened to him. Everything became for him your *darshan*."

"Yes."

"This seeing reverses everything. It reveals pain to be joy, death to be life, humiliation to be opportunity, horror to be the chance for the new truth."

"It changes everything," she confirmed.

"What is needed," Ma said after a silence, "is the awareness at all moments of Unity. From that comes love and truth and divine power."

I rocked slightly in the bliss streaming from her body.

"Every day with you," I said to her, "my wonder grows."

"Wonder," she repeated, saying the word slowly, playfully. "Did I say it the right way?"

"Yes." I laughed. I had heard ONE-DER.

That evening there was no *darshan* so my lesson with Ma took place with her in her work clothes. She had a green pen mark on her forehead.

Adilakshmi watched us with a rag tied around her face because of a toothache. When Adilakshmi was in the kitchen preparing fruit juice, I asked Ma, "You are removing the last barriers between us, aren't you?"

She nodded and looked down.

Then she said, "The Goddess has many masks she needs in Her play."

Her face changed and became the burning face of the Goddess. The air blazed around her. For a moment I was terrified. Then I said, "But your final face is the face of love."

Ma said softly, "In Telugu we have a song: 'Love can melt the stone, can turn the mountain to water.' "

"A Persian poet wrote," I said softly, " 'The moth flies into the candle and is burned away.' "

"The candle itself is burning away," said Ma. "Both moth and candle are only fire."

There was a rose on the table in front of Ma. I saw that it was almost open. Our eyes met over it.

Two days of fierce purification followed.

*From my notebook:*

I am being made to see exactly the nature of my vanity as a writer and would-be "communicator" of her Truth. I see that to believe myself her instrument is another trap for the ego. Just at the moment I feel empowered to begin to think about beginning to write, I am made to see how vain some of my motives for writing about her still are.

I am disgusted with the whole idea of writing anything. I feel terrified at myself, terrified at the way I might yet deform the experience by writing about it, terrified of betraying her by telling her truth in a garbled or vain way.

I watch this terror and disgust and know they come from her and are necessary.

*Nothing can be done in the old way.*

*You cannot walk or talk or eat or move or write in the old way.*

Today I read in Aurobindo: "To regard oneself as an instrument of the Divine is not a perfect remedy, for when a strong ego meddles in this matter it falsifies the spiritual relation and under cover of making itself an instrument of the

Divine is really bent on making God instead an instrument. The one remedy is to still the egoistic claim of whatever kind . . . to let the Shakti lay hold of us and use us for the divine purpose."

*You will have to die to be able to write about me,* I heard her say. *You will only be able to write about me 'posthumously.'*

 Ma was sitting by the table again. The roses had opened by the time I went to teach her English the next evening.

This time Ma began the conversation. "J came to me and said 'I do not want to desire anything, even God.' I said, 'You must desire God.' He said he had read many books that told him all desire was wrong. I said that the desire for God ended all other desire. He said he did not think so. What can I do?

"Even avatars," she went on, "have to desire to be in God at every moment. And when avatars die, they desire with all their being to be united with God. The greatest beings, like Aurobindo, go on desiring God more and more deeply, right until the end of their lives."

"So, realization does not mean the end of desire?" I asked. "It means the beginning of the true desire, the desire that comes out of union for an ever deeper Union?"

"Yes." Ma looked at the roses, smiling. "How much desire there has to be for the roses to open completely. Look at Ramakrishna. How much he wept and prayed for the Divine Mother!"

Ma gazed at me.

"A tear," she said, "is a door through which I can come. How can I come into a heart that does not long for me?"

Then she said quietly, "Be careful now. Be very careful."

ॐ The next evening at *darshan* as I gazed into her eyes fire blazed from them and my body fell away like sand.

Afterward I put my face in my hands and swore that never, in any life, would I forget her face as I saw it in those moments—blazing with diamond Light, fierce with absolute will.

She was wearing white, the white of Unity.

A mantra was given inwardly for my journey: *More and more love and more surrender.*

Twenty minutes later, trembling, I went up to "teach" her English.

Adilakshmi opened the door.

Ma sat smiling tenderly on the sofa, stilll in the white sari, but small and girlish now.

She knew how shaken I had been and treated me with exquisite gentleness.

We finished the next lesson in the English book quietly, and then she looked at me.

"You have some questions, no?"

"It is harder than ever to speak tonight," I said. "I am drunk on you."

"Then, drink some fruit juice," she said, smiling, handing me a glass full of orange juice.

Curling my fingers around the cool glass, I said: "Each of my senses has been awakened by your Light into a new dimension. You are awakening me to a Mind—what Aurobindo calls the supermind, I suppose—and this Mind sees and does not think, knows and does not have opinions."

"Yes. It is like that."

"This mind sees in clusters. It hears Reality like music."

"Yes."

"Everything I have lived with you has always been like this. Only now I am beginning to see it."

Ma nodded, waiting, gazing at me.

"If I had known at the beginning what I know now, I would have been frightened."

Ma laughed. "You could not know at the beginning. Knowledge can come only from experience. What do words and ideas mean? They are only useful when you have had the experience."

"Or to inspire others to seek it."

Ma nodded.

I looked at Ma and cleared my throat.

"At the end of *darshan* tonight I saw your body as immense—a body of quietly moving white light. The movement was very soft."

"Once when Mr. Reddy was sick I visited him in the hospital and he saw me as a great fountain of golden light, shaped like a mango. That, too, is one of my bodies."

I smiled because Ma said it as she would describe a walk or a visit to the market.

"How do you bear the light in and around you?"

"This body is used to it."

"Weren't you frightened in the beginning, as a child, when the light began to possess your body?"

"No." She laughed. "As a child I used to love going out alone into the dark. People said it was dangerous, that there were scorpions everywhere. But it never frightened me."

I thought of her as a small, thin girl with huge eyes and pigtails going out alone into the dark of a village in Andhra Pradesh.

"How alone you must have been, with no one who could possibly understand what was happening to you."

Ma looked quietly down.

Then she asked, "How is the book?"

It was the first time she had ever asked about the book.

She was looking at me amusedly.

I heard myself say, "I realize I cannot begin until you have given me a sign, until this Process is over."

Ma nodded.

"Will you give me that sign soon?"

Ma nodded.

Suddenly the image came to me of a vast spiral, narrowing to a glowing center and then emerging again, but transformed, filled with the Light of the Center.

And with the image came a clear understanding that Ma was taking all my senses into that center, through all the spirals of mystic experience, and that, when I had reached and been through its center, I would be able to reenact in words what I had undergone, illumined by her Knowledge. I told Ma what I had realized.

Ma nodded. "It will be like that. In one way you will never finish the book."

I groaned. "Oh, Ma, don't say that. If you say that, I will never even begin."

She turned to me gravely.

"There is no end to divine work. Your work will not end with the book. Your life will be your book."

Ma poured me another orange juice.

"Here," she said. "Drink the rest."

The next night a soft glory of quiet light surrounded Ma after *darshan*. We sat alone again on the sofa. She wore the red-and-white sari she had worn for *darshan*. The strength of her presence was so great, I could not speak for a long time.

Adilakshmi came in and sat down. That evening she, too, was more beautiful than I had ever seen her, in a gold-and-green sari.

"I feel," I said to her," as if tonight we are in the divine world with Ma."

Adilakshmi smiled. "It is like that sometimes."

I took off the ring I wear on my marriage finger and gave it to Ma.

It has three bands, of different types of gold—reddish, yellow, white.

She smiled, held up the ring by the white band, blessed it silently, and gave it back.

# TWELVE

That night, the twenty-ninth of November, I dreamed of walking with Mr. Reddy on the sands of Mahabalipuram.

We were laughing and holding hands, like children.

He said, "Take your shirt off. You will be surprised."

I took my shirt off. On my left side I had grown one perfect breast.

"Now you are two-in-one," Mr. Reddy said.

A friend from Paris phoned early the next morning, and I ran up the stairs to take the call. Ma was dressed and ready to go out shopping with W.

"Would you like to come?" she asked gently.

I nodded, took the call quickly, and raced down the stairs to find her still alone, sitting, putting on her boots.

These boots always make me smile; they are faintly "cowboy" and have small leather tassels that hang down.

Later, as Adilakshmi went to the dentist with W, I found myself in the car alone with Ma in the parking lot at Hadamar.

I was sitting in the back where I could watch Ma's face as she gazed out at the morning. It was ageless; peaceful. The image rose in my mind of a Javanese sculpture of *Prajna paramita*, Supreme Wisdom of Emptiness, that I loved. I looked at Ma's eyes looking out at the morning, and my body also filled with their silence.

"Human beings," I said, "can do nothing without God, can they?"

"In India we have a saying: 'Not even an ant can move without the grace of God.' "

The others arrived and we drove to Massa, the supermarket.

Ma put me into a light trance. Wandering through the rows of pickled cucumbers and tomatoes in Massa became a secretly hilarious experience. Even the canned music seemed sweet.

I watched Ma shopping, which she does as calmly and soberly as she does everything else. She moved around Massa as if she owned it, aware of where everything was, testing the fruit and vegetables like any shrewd housewife, bending down to see the exact prices and noting them carefully. Daniel had often described Ma's scrupulous frugality with some hilarity, but now I saw for myself.

Afterward we stood together in the crisp sunlit cold.

Suddenly I saw Ma's eyes concentrate. A minute later she was twenty yards away, fetching a grocery cart for two bewildered old people lost in the concrete wilderness outside the shop.

I had been concentrating so on her that I did not notice their grief. She had been aware of everyone around her.

We watched the two old people walk arm in arm into the supermarket with the shopping cart and Ma turned to me, her face alight with humor.

Then we drove to a car wash nearby.

As we were passing through two enormous washers, both Durga-red, the car filled with her power and bliss. Ma in the front seat took photos of me and Adilakshmi in the backseat.

Her voice: *You have been photographing me all these months for your film. Now you are in mine.*

She was more playful than I had ever seen her, like a small girl.

As the great red car washers covered the windows and filled the car with red light, Ma sat laughing and clicking away on the camera.

The scene and its strange power has returned to me again and again in meditation and in dreams: Ma laughing, the great red washers, the sound of the camera.

The trance that had begun in Massa now deepened.

"What now?" I asked her, when the car had been cleaned.

She laughed, "Now we go to Limburg Cathedral."

There was no one else in the cathedral when we got there except a group of priests at the altar singing chants to the Virgin Mary. Ma went immediately to a chapel on the side to light candles to Christ and the Virgin. She stood by me as I tried to light mine and failed several times. Taking the candle from me, she placed it squarely on its stand. She kept her hands around it to ensure it stayed steady.

I knew what she was showing me.

Her candle and mine stood side by side where she had placed them, their flames almost touching, burning calmly.

"You have awakened and lit my soul, Ma," I said to her. "Keep it burning."

She nodded and moved to the back of the church, where she sat, almost out of sight behind a pillar.

Her voice: *It will burn now until the end.*

The priests in white sang about the splendors and virtues of the Virgin. A great medieval crucifix of Christ hung in the middle of the church. Several times I saw the Divine Light appear and glow around it.

I was sitting with W in front of Ma and Adilakshmi. Once I turned to look at Ma, but her face was as impassive as in *darshan*, her hands folded in the same way in her lap.

Slowly my body and spirit filled with the power emanating from her.

Each ancient and glorious phrase the priests sang in praise of Mary my soul sang in praise of Ma.

The words came, as I gazed at the crucifix glowing in divine light: *Make me like He who hangs there, Mother, your child of absolute love.*

*Expand my heart so the whole world is in it always.*

Her voice, calmly and clearly:

*Those who love the world serve it.*

*Soon it will be time to return to the world*

*to share what you have been given.*

I saw the Divine Light grow in the nave of the church and cover the moving bodies of the priests and the gold stone pillars of the church, grow and breathe, as if in unison with the chanting, then slowly vanish.

The service ended. Ma remained in her seat for several minutes as if collecting herself and then got up to leave. She walked on ahead of us, into the starlit dark outside.

No one said anything on the drive back.

Before going to sleep I opened to a page of Aurobindo: "Divine Love should lead to the perfect Knowledge of the Beloved by perfect intimacy, thus becoming a path of Knowledge, *and to divine service*, thus becoming a path of works."

The next night I asked Ma, "Is the condition on which the Mother gives Children the Power, the Shakti, that they then devote it to working for her in the world, with others and for others?"

"Yes, they must work completely for others! This is what will make them most happy."

She looked at the one open red rose in front of her.

"The center must be in God. Then the flower can go on and on opening outward."

"For that, divine strength is needed."

"It will be given." She looked down. Then she bent over the rose gently and smelled it.

🕉 I had to return to Paris two days later to talk to a director who wanted to make a film of one of my novels. I felt more forlorn than at any other stage of my journey with Ma. My apartment seemed dowdy and cold, the city unreal. The conversations with the director foundered in banal financial wrangling. My whole being ached for Ma in a way it had never done, viscerally, with physical suffering. My dreams were full of images of collapse, houses burning, seas of blood, old lovers deriding everything I had done.

Peace came only when I was alone and concentrated on her. In those hours I slowly realized I was entering a kind of communion with her more absolute than any I had enjoyed, even in her presence, even at *darshan*. As my old life collapsed around me the new life she had given me grew stronger than ever.

🕉 Astrid: "Your journey is coming to an end. She is seeing to it that there is nothing in your spirit now but Her."

Astrid stood up and started pacing her room. Then she stopped, looking at me. "The last part of the climb is the hardest. Everything comes up to try and stop you climbing the final sheer rock-face. Doubts, madnesses, of all kinds. Laugh at them."

She came close to me and took my head in her hands. "Every time you come back from her you are different. This time you are definitively different. You are growing her eyes. That is the sign."

Then I told Astrid what had happened in the Metro on my way to dinner. "I left my apartment at about seven feeling helpless. I felt I had failed Ma in not being able to reenter my life in Paris happily. I felt it was absurd even to think of writing a book about the Journey at a time like this. My dreams recently have been full of cynical voices. Every time I walk in the streets I see everything that is ranged against vision of any kind. I was sitting slumped in gloom thinking I would not be able to write anything when all at once I felt two hands grabbing my lapels.

"A beautiful drunk boy was staring into my eyes. Do you know what he said, and in English, in front of all the other people in the carriage who were looking at us? 'You must believe," he said, 'you must believe.' "

That night when I returned to my apartment I meditated an hour and went deep, closing my eyes. When I opened them, the photo of Ma in front of me was blazing.

*Look around the room.*

As I looked, all the photos of all the avatars and saints I have in my room—Aurobindo, Ramakrishna, Ramana Maharshi, Anandamayi Ma—began to radiate light, Ma's outlines appearing imposed on each of them.

ॐ Three days later I told Astrid: "The Light is always there now. I have only to concentrate on her face and the Light begins. Whenever I look into Ramakrishna's eyes, or Aurobindo's, the Light is also there. Today I saw Aurobindo's pale blue Light for the first time."

"When the Light is always there," Astrid said after a long pause, "you are approaching Unity."

I reminisced: "In one of our last conversations I gave Ma this ring," I held up my left hand, displaying the ring made of three hues of gold.

"And she held it up by the white gold?" Astrid lit a cigarette, amused.

"How did you know?"

"Ma is dissolving herself for you into the Light where you both come from. She is curing you of the last parts of your idolatry—necessary though it was—of her physical self so you can enter into her eternal self, which is the Light, the Brahman." She paused. "Supreme Masters like her take you beyond themselves, beyond your relationship with even the ecstasies they give you, into this Unity, where you are one with them in the Light they are one with. Afterward you return to duality, but now you know always where and who you and everyone else is."

I meditated all the next day and evening, not moving from my chair, listening to the birds in my courtyard, gazing into the faces of all my Guides and Friends, now illumined at all moments.

About midnight I wandered into the Parisian night.

As I was about to go back into the courtyard of my apartment building, I saw a chair in the antiques shop opposite that amused me by its grace and beauty. Its back was a large perfect circle that, I thought, contained a mirror. What a witty conceit, I thought, as I walked toward it impelled by a surprising force, a chair with a mirror for its back!

I walked toward the chair and looked in the mirror.

What happened then is hard to describe. I felt hit from outside by a crowbar of Light on my skull, and my skull split open.

There was no mirror.

My eyes fell through the mirror I had thought was there and laughingly expanded to gather in the whole room, the whole street, everything around it.

My legs gave way, and I sat on the pavement, laughing loudly. It had been the most perfect, the most transcendent of all her jokes.

The "mirror" had been in the shape of my ring that I had given her to be blessed. The wood of the frame was white.

*No "you" or "I." No reflection. Only That.*

*No "you" or "I." Only the eternal light.*

The laughter shook my body. It came from a deeper, wilder place than I had ever known before and shook my whole self like a storm shakes a tree. The entire street, wet with rain; the shop; the chair; the shiny sleek tops of the cars; the peeling khaki door of my courtyard—all seemed also to be laughing, glittering and laughing.

At the other end of the street, an old clochard was scavenging in one of the large red plastic garbage cans. He turned and saw me laughing, sitting in the rain, smiled and tweaked his cap.

I went into my courtyard. The walls of the building were dancing in Her Fire, like starlit smoke. Everything was dancing in time with everything else, the walls, the windows, the stars, my dirty wet hands, my mind.

*One dance. One dance. One dance.*

Somehow I walked up the stairs to my room.

I went in, not turning on the light.

*Turn and look in the mirror.*

There is a mirror all along the small wall above my bed.

I turned.

I was not in the mirror. There was only a Dance in the mirror, only a light hilarious spiral of drunken leaping atoms, a Dance of Fire in which everything was swirling—the bedspread, the chair, my hands moving up and down, the strict classical railings of the outside window.

All was Myself, dancing in Fire in Myself. Then a Peace descended, of which I remember nothing.

ॐ When I returned to Thalheim on Christmas Eve, I found Ma fixing the lighting outside the kitchen.

I stood gazing at her. She smiled and said, "Have you seen your room?"

"No. I came straight to you."

I had brought for Ma a statue of Ganesh and a painting of Kali and went unsteadily to give them to her. She was coming up the stairs from the kitchen, slowly, gazing upward, radiant with Divine Light.

I gave her the Ganesh without saying anything. I had bought it in Mahabalipuram.

Ma took it and cradled it in her hands.

"I love Ganesh," she said softly. "He is delicate."

I remembered the statue she had made out of ice the winter before, looking out over Thalheim and the world.

Send him to me, I prayed inwardly.

She followed me into my room and stood, glowing and silent, as I handed her the painting of Kali, standing over Shiva, with a row of skulls around her neck.

"You are wearing the skulls," I said, "like a necklace of pearls. Here I am," I said smiling, pointing to one of them. "Wear me always."

"She is very peaceful," Ma said, gazing at herself at Kali.

She looked down raptly at the carpet, closing her eyes a little.

I gave her the other presents I had brought for her—a black box with a gold painting inside its lid, a book of poems I had written years ago for her, illustrated in tropical colors by a friend.

"Is this all for me?" she said, in a light, wondering voice.

"You have given me my true life. You have shown me my divine being. I am yours . . ." My voice trailed away.

She bowed her head.

We stood silently and then she left the room.

The next day, Christmas Day, nine years after I had met her for the first time, when I went to have breakfast, I saw her sitting on the stairs outside the door alone, very quiet, putting on her boots.

I sat on the stairs beside her.

"You have been my Mother in all ways, and my Master, and my Beloved, and my Friend."

She gazed at me.

"When I gave you my ring to bless . . ." I could not finish.

"Yes, I blessed the ring," she said.

"In Paris you gave me the Brahman experience, the experience of Unity," I said, the words sounding ridiculous.

She nodded.

"It is the end of this journey." I went on, "There will be many more journeys. But the one begun nine years ago in time is over. The ones in eternity are just beginning."

She nodded, bending down to adjust her right boot.

"In Paris," I said, "I knew all things were myself, dancing in Light, Your Light, My Light. I knew myself a divine part of You, your Child. I knew these things by the Light of Knowledge itself. I was the experience and I was understanding the Experience from within Your Mind, seeing with Your eyes."

She smiled.

"This will become stable," she said.

We sat quietly.

"Do not be attached to any experience," she said, "however great."

"That is why you cleaned my room, isn't it? To show me

that I must not be attached to the Joy you showed me in Paris, to show me that I must, like you, love, accept, and serve the world."

"You are the world," she said. "You cannot reap the gifts of the Divine and not also do the Work."

Her smile broadened.

"All worlds are here. You must be in all the worlds at once."

She stood up, smoothing her hair back from her forehead.

"Everything you think or do," Ma went on, "you must dedicate to the world in love. Live in the eternal but waste no time. Everything you do for love of the world, you do for Me. Everything you do for Me, you do for your true Self. There is no separation between you and Me and the world. Now you know that."

She paused to adjust her left boot and continued: "If you use Knowledge to escape Reality, you are in another prison."

We stood in silence, gazing at each other.

"Save the world as you have saved me," I whispered.

She nodded and went out calmly into the garden.


Three days followed in which, hour after hour, minute after minute, in calm, unbroken trance, the joys and revelations Ma had given me returned in faultless sequence and with a splendor strengthened by my recognition of where they had culminated—in the gift She gave me in Paris of the constant conscious presence of the Divine Light, of the cosmic presence of the Divine Mother.

This Light and Presence have never left me and grow stronger. Through all the fears and ordeals of these last two years; through the long, often painful struggle to be clear enough to write this book; through my continuing battle with all that is vain, closed, perverse, and lazy in myself, the Light of the Mother has burned consciously in my mind and in the creation before me, to inspire and humble me and remind me, at each moment, even when I did not want to be reminded, of the divine identity of myself and all beings. I have not stopped suffering, but doubt has gone. My desires, anxieties, and ambitions have not disappeared, but they are ghostly to me, and I am no longer driven by them. The process of dying scares me; but death itself does not. Through Her grace, I have lived in my deep Self for long stretches of time and know It cannot die. Taken out of the world to be taught what I have related here, I have returned to the world to give and do what I can and am coming to know, slowly and soberly, Her hope and Her joy in every activity.

On New Year's Day I saw Ma walking alone up the street outside my window. I went out of my room and walked up to her. We stood smiling in silence.

"The Child is a dolphin," I said, making wavy motions with my hands. "A dolphin always at play in the sea of the Mother's Mind."

Ma laughed.

"Yes, the dolphin is wise and free and full of humor." She turned to go.

"There is so much for humanity to learn, Ma," I said. "And despite everything, we can learn it. I know that now."

Ma turned back silently, gazing into my eyes.

*To give humanity time is why I am here.*

Six days later, on January sixth, the night of the feast of Epiphany, I had this dream:

I was walking with Ma in a spring landscape, rocky and vibrant, like the landscape around Delphi. She walked on ahead through olive groves and meadows full of flowers I had never seen before, brilliant and fragrant. Every so often she would turn to see if I was following.

We reached a path winding up a steep cliff.

*Close your eyes*, I heard her say within me, *and go on walking.*

I closed my eyes and continued, sometimes stumbling painfully, but never resting or opening my eyes.

*You can open your eyes now.*

I was on the top of the cliff, looking out over the sea. There, from one side of the horizon to another, the sea was full of dolphins, leaping in the dawn air, wild with their cries of joy. Above them, in a vast red sun, was Ma's face, smiling the same smile of triumph as she had exactly nine years before, when, at that first Epiphany in the doorway of her house in Pondicherry, she began to shatter my life open.

# ACKNOWLEDGMENTS

To Adilakshmi, for all her help and the inspiration of her devotion to Ma.

To Amy Hertz and Christie Cox for their brilliant and brave editing.

To Jeff Cox for his loyalty and hospitality.

To Susan Henderson, Fred Weiner, Bo and Cat Carlson, and Lourdes Brache for their exemplary typing of the finished manuscript.

To Frances Coady and Liz Calder, for their tireless encouragement.

To Bokara Patterson, Marie Jaoul de Poncheville, and Lavinia Currier for their friendship.

BOOKS ON THE MOTHER

*The Mother* by Adilakshmi

*Bringing Down the Light: Journey of a Soul after Death*, (Meeramma, Ithaca, NY)

*The Way of the Divine Mother: Questions and Answers* by Mother Meera (Meeramma, Ithaca, NY)

PAINTING BY MOTHER MEERA